ID: The True You

Mark Batterson

Contents

⟡

Preface

✦⇒◉⇐✦

When you meet someone for the first time it's like opening a book to page 317 and beginning to read. It's tough to put page 317 in context because you haven't read page 267 or 112 or 15. This book isn't a biography, but let me give you some personal history so you can put the book in context.

I will have made thirty-five trips around the sun by the time this book is first published. I was born in Minneapolis, Minnesota but grew up in Naperville, Illinois a western suburb of Chicago. I'm a denominational mutt having gone to seven different church brands growing up. I began my college career at the University of Chicago as a pre-law major, but ended up pursuing ministry after a prayer walk through a cow pasture in August of 1989 (that's the short version). I've been married to my wife, Lora, for twelve years and we have three children—Parker, Summer, and Josiah. I've pastored National Community Church in Washington, DC since the blizzard of '96. And I can honestly say that I wouldn't want to be anyplace else doing anything else with anyone else.

In one sense, I feel qualified to write on this topic

because of my personal, parental, and pastoral experience. But in another sense, I don't think you ever feel qualified to put the last period on the page. I'm a recovering perfectionist which makes it even tougher because I'm never satisfied. It's tough for me to tie off the umbilical cord, but I do it in hopes that this book will live and breathe and take on a life of its own.

My goal in writing is simple: I want you to see yourself the way God sees you.

Your identity depends on it.

Prologue

◦·⇒◦⇐·◦

Your **self-concept**—the way you see yourself—**is determined by what you base your identity on.** And you have lots of choices.

You can base your identity on how you look. You can base your identity on what you do or how much you make doing it. You can base your identity on titles or degrees or resumes. You can even base your identity on what you wear or what you drive. As crazy as it sounds, you know it's true. Some people define themselves by the brand of clothing they wear or the model of car they drive. There are a million factors that comprise our self-concept, but all of us base our identity on something.

Driving Mr. Albert is a fascinating book about Thomas Harvey, the pathologist who performed the autopsy on Albert Einstein in 1955. It's pretty bizarre, but Thomas Harvey kept Einstein's brain in a Tupperware bowl in his home for forty years! Einstein's brain became the locus of Harvey's identity. One of the interviewees said, "That brain is his entire identity." The book ends with Thomas Harvey giving the brain to Dr. Elliot Krauss at Princeton Hospital and it's almost like Harvey is a free man for the first time in forty years! He's no longer defined by the brain. He is finally free to be himself.

We can base our identity on some pretty bizarre things, but all of us base our identity on something—consciously or subconsciously. **Identity problems are simply the byproduct of basing your identity on the wrong thing.**

ID Problems

I have a theory. It may seem counterintuitive at first, but I think it's true. **The more you have going for you the more potential you have for identity problems.** Here's why. It's easier for you to base your identity on the wrong thing—how good you look, how much you have, or how successful you are.

In a recent interview, singer-songwriter Michael Card talked about a counseling experience he had a few years ago. He said the biggest discovery he made was that his gift wasn't his identity. He said, "If it is, I'm an idolater." For too many people their gift becomes their identity. Michael Card said, "The greatest impediment to spiritual intimacy is your giftedness."

If anything is going to undermine your reliance upon God and become a source of pride in your life it's going to be your gift. So the more you have going for you the more potential you have for identity problems because it's easier for you to base your identity on the wrong thing. You reduce yourself to how you look, what you have, or what you do. But you are so much more than that!

My goal in writing this book is pretty simple and straightforward—I want you see yourself the way God sees you. Romans 12:3 says, **"The only accurate way to understand ourselves is by what God is and what he does for us"** (*The Message*).

As a follower of Christ, I find my identity in Christ. My identity is not based on **who I am** or **what I can do.** My identity is based on **who Christ is** and **what Christ has done for me.**

Time Before Time

Let me hit the rewind button and take you back to time before time. Ezekiel 28 is a prologue to human history. Before God created the heavens and the earth there was mutiny in heaven. The coup d'etat was instigated by an angel named Lucifer. And the fall of Lucifer predates the fall of man.

Ezekiel 28 is an instant replay of exactly what happened. You can almost detect a touch of regret in God's voice. "I ordained and anointed you as the mighty angelic guardian. You had access to the holy mountain of God and walked among the stones of fire."

It's a cryptic description, but what's clear is that Lucifer enjoyed the unadulterated presence of God. Verse 12 says he was "the perfection of wisdom and beauty." Lucifer had everything going for him, but that wasn't enough. Verse 17 says, "Your heart became proud on account of your beauty, and you corrupted your wisdom because of your splendor."

Let me say it as concisely as I can: all suffering, all evil, all brokenness, all pain are the aftereffects of a chain reaction that can be traced all the way back to this one moment in time before time when Lucifer rebelled. It is the original sin. Lucifer had everything going for him. He was beautiful. He was wise. He was powerful. But enough wasn't enough. And therein lies the eternal challenge: the more you have going for you the more potential you have for identity problems because it's easier for you to base your identity on the wrong thing—who you are instead of the God who made you who you are.

That is the genesis of pride and the reason for Lucifer's rebellion. Instead of worshipping the God who made him beautiful and wise, Lucifer wanted to be worshipped.

In his book, *Epic*, John Eldredge says, "There is a danger for the glorious that the humble will never know; a trial for the powerful that the weak will never face. You see this in the worst of the dictators, the Hitlers and Stalins, the Maos and Amins—they set themselves up to be idols. They want more than power; they want to be worshipped."

That is the beginning of the end spiritually.

ID Crisis

If you base your identity on the wrong things you're building a house of cards. To put it in biblical language, basing your identity on who you are or what you can do is like building your house on the sand. Jesus said, "The rain came down, the streams rose, the wind blew and beat against the house, and it fell with a great crash."

The crash goes by a few different names depending on the stage of life. If you're in your twenties it's called a quarterlife crisis. If you're approaching halftime, it's called a midlife crisis. It doesn't get much attention, but I think there is a fourth-quarter crisis right around the time the kids leave home or you retire.

Here's what happens. You base your identity on school and then you graduate. You base your identity on a spouse and they file for divorce. You base your identity on a job and you get downsized or retire. You base your identity on your kids and they leave home. Schools, marriages, jobs, kids—those are good things. But you can't base your identity on them.

In high school and college, my life revolved around basketball. I played two hours a day every day. I felt good when I had a good game. I felt bad when I had a bad game. Basketball was a huge part of my identity, but here's the thing. I didn't get drafted. The NBA doesn't do much recruiting at Central Bible College. I waited by the phone on draft day, but they must have dialed the wrong number! One way of looking at it is this: when my basketball career ended part of me died—the part that based its identity on basketball.

That is what happens anytime you go through a major life change. One chapter begins and another ends. It's normal to feel a mixture of sadness and joy on your graduation day or wedding day or moving day or retirement day because there is loss in gain.

When you get married it's wonderful, but the single person dies.

When you graduate from school it's wonderful, but the student dies.

When you accomplish a goal it's wonderful, but the goal dies.

When you turn twenty it's wonderful, but the teenager dies.

When you retire it's wonderful, but the vocation dies.

Why is there an inexplicable sadness behind the smile on graduation day? Why is there is a twinge of sadness when you say goodbye to family on your wedding day or colleagues on your retirement day? Why is there is a let down after accomplishing a goal? It's pretty simple: there is loss in gain. It's normal to grieve the graduation or wedding or goal or birthday or retirement. Part of you dies.

Quarterlife Crisis

I pastor a congregation that is the inverse of most churches. National Community Church is 80% single and 80% twenty-something. Most NCCers are headed towards, in the middle of, or coming out of a quarterlife crisis. Some of life's most critical decisions will be made during the third decade of life: what to do, where to live, who to marry. **We make most of our major decisions during our twenties and we spend the rest of our lives managing those major decisions!**

Under the surface, there is a shifting of the tectonic plates during our twenties. We make the transition from the world of school to the world of work. During the first quarter of life, our identity (for better or for worse) is based on school. And the better student you were or the more involved in extracurricular activities or the more you enjoyed school the harder it is to make that transition. I prolonged my transition with two graduates programs!

It's a taboo topic for twenty-somethings, but graduating from school can be pretty scary and pretty lonely. Why? Because you have to start all over again! Your identity is based on something other than school or school-related activities for the first time in your life. Of course, your identity shouldn't be based on your GPA to begin with.

Self-Choice

At some point each of us has to make a choice and it's the most important choice that any of us will ever make. You have to choose between you and God.

C.S. Lewis said, "There are only two kinds of people in the end: those who say to God, 'Thy will be done,' and those to whom God says, in the end, 'Thy will be done.' All that are in Hell, choose it. Without that self-choice there could be no Hell."

Here's what is so tricky about that choice. We mistakenly think that the way to find fulfillment and happiness is to live for ourselves. But if you live for yourself you'll end up a miserable person because it's not what you were created to do. Here's the problem with worshipping yourself. If you're anything like me, you run out of stuff to worship real quick! You weren't created to worship you. You were created to worship the God who created you!

We mistakenly think that living for God will somehow narrow our lives, but it infinitely expands our horizons. In the words of A.W. Tozer, "**Eternity won't be long enough to**

learn all that God is or praise Him for all He has done."
There is a great dialogue at the end of *Prince Caspian*,
the second book in *The Chronicles of Narnia* series by C.S.
Lewis. The children haven't seen Aslan in a long time and
one of the girls says, "Aslan, you're bigger." He says, "That
is because you are older, little one." She says, "Not because
you are bigger?" Aslan says, "I am not. But every year you
grow, you will find me bigger."
And so it is in our relationship with God: **the more we
grow the bigger God gets!**
Psalm 34:3 says, "Magnify the Lord with me, and let us
exalt his name together." The word "magnify" means "to get
bigger and bigger." That's a microcosm of spiritual growth:
God gets bigger and bigger. And as God gets bigger and
bigger our problems become smaller and smaller. Tozer
said, "**A low view of God entertained almost universally
among Christians is the cause of a hundred lesser evils.**"
But the man with a **high view** of God "**is relieved of ten
thousand temporal problems.**"
You have a choice to make: are you going to base your
identity on who you are—how you look, what you have,
what you do? Or are you going to base your identity on who
God is and what God can do? That choice will determine
who you become.
I sense a seismic shift in my life. It's the only thing that
qualifies my writing. It started with a single thought during
forty days of prayer and fasting this past summer: **too many
of us base our identity on what we can do for God
instead of basing our identity on what God can do for us.**
That one thought has totally revolutionized what I see
when I look in the mirror. I have found such freedom and
joy and rest in the simple fact that my identity is not based
on what I can do for God, but on what God has done, can
do, and will do for me. So much of my life has been based
on personal performance—how I did in school, how I did on

the basketball court, how I did in the pulpit. But I'm learning to base more and more of my identity on who God is and what God can do and less and less of my identity on who I am and what I can do.

Almost like a daily reminder in *Microsoft Outlook*, this thought pops up on a daily basis: **it's not about what I can do for God; it's about what God has done for me.**

I'm a child of God. I'm a temple of the Holy Spirit. My sins are nailed to the cross. My name is written in the Lamb's book of life. I didn't do any of that. God did it for me.

Act I: The Miracle

Every life is a miracle of immeasurable proportions

George Shaffner

There never has been and never will be anyone like you. That isn't a testament to you. It's a testament to the God who created you.

Uniqueness isn't a virtue. Hitler was uniquely evil. All of us have done uniquely dumb things! The significance of uniqueness is this: **no one else can worship God like you**. No one can take your place. You are invaluable and irreplaceable.

One in a Jillion Gazillion

◆━━◎◯━━◆

To really understand who you are you need to know **where you come from** and **where you're headed**. Let me put it in philosophical terms. Causality asks the question: where do we come from? Teleology asks the question: where are we headed? How you answer the causalogical and teleological questions will determine how you look at life and look at yourself.

When it comes to causality you really only have two choices: either you are the byproduct of **random chance** or **intelligent design**. My generation overdosed on Darwin. Much of our angst is the subconscious result of being taught that we are accidents descended from apes or amoeba. If you really believe that, it's an epistemological parasite that eventually sucks the meaning out of life.

In *On the Origin of the Species*, Charles Darwin said, "Man with all his noble qualities still bears in his bodily frame the indelible stamp of his lowly origin."

I couldn't agree with anything less.

We are anything but accidents!

1 in 10^{40,000}

Sir Fred Hoyle, one of the world's leading astronomers was speaking at the *British Academy of Science* several years ago. He said, "Let's be scientifically honest. The probability of life arising to greater and greater complexity by chance through evolution is the same probability as having a tornado tear through a junkyard and form a Boeing 747 jetliner." He calculated the chances of life being the result of random chance as being 1 in 10 ^{40,000}.

I don't have enough faith to believe in random chance!

The most complicated clock in the world is the Jens Olsen astronomical clock in Copenhagen, Denmark. The clock took more than forty years to build at a cost of more than a million dollars. It has ten faces and 15,000 parts. The clock computes the time of day, the days of the week, the months and years and the movements of the planets for 2500 years and is accurate to 2/5th of a second every 300 years. What's even more amazing is that some of the 15,000 parts in the clock will not move for twenty-five centuries.

Now let me ask you a question: If a tourist taking a tour of Copenhagen asked a tour guide who made the clock and that tour guide told him that nobody made the clock, in fact, about forty years earlier there was an explosion (a big bang) in Copenhagen and all of a sudden the 15,000 parts that makeup the clock starting working together in perfect synchronization, would any logical person believe him?

Of course not. Why not? Because as human beings we have the ability to recognize something that is the result of intelligent design.

Albert Einstein said, **"There are only two ways to live your life. One is as if nothing is a miracle. The other is as if everything is."**

You aren't an accident.

You're nothing short of a miracle!

23,000 Thank Yous

The Psalmist said, "I praise you because I am fearfully and wonderfully made."

If you could unravel your body like a ball of yarn, there would be enough DNA-string to reach the moon and back ten thousand times! A hundred things are happening in your body right now and you don't give it a second-thought—breathing, digesting, growing new cells, purifying toxins, maintaining hormonal balance, converting storied energy from fat to blood sugar, and repairing damaged cells. Approximately six trillion reactions are taking place in every cell every second. Your heart will pump 100,000 times today without skipping a beat. Touch your nose with your finger. Go ahead. No one is looking. That simple act required four hundred separate chemical reactions firing across tens of thousands of synapses.

In *The Miracle of Breath*, James Robinson says, "Consider the journey of an oxygen atom. The same atom, which at this moment hovers around your nostrils, was once in the lungs of a dinosaur."

The journey begins when air passes through your nose where unwanted dust and debris is filtered out. For what it's worth, the average person moves about 440 cubic feet of air every day! You ought to have a sense of accomplishment at the end of each day! The oxygen atom travels through the trachea into the lungs. The surface area of your lungs is forty times greater than the surface area of your entire body—all compressed within the tiny confines between your ribs. The oxygen atom then hitchhikes with hemoglobin and travels throughout the entire human body via blood vessels. If those blood vessels were laid end to end they would be approximately 100,000 miles long. The blood vessels in your body could wrap around the equator four times! At the end of the journey, oxygen enters individual cells, bonds with the food we eat and releases energy.

Biologists call it cellular respiration. I'd call it a miracle! "Webster's Dictionary defines a miracle as 'an extraordinary, unusual wonder or marvel'," Robinson writes. "Isn't a bloodstream 100,000 miles long, in a small body, an unusual wonder? Isn't the journey of an oxygen atom a true marvel? We don't need supernatural events to experience a miracle. All we need is breath. The human breath is Sacred. Cherish your breathing: it is the miraculous gift of life."

The average person takes approximately 23,000 breaths per day. Translation: we owe God approximately 23,000 thank you's every single day! Job 34:14 says, "If it were his intention and he withdrew his spirit and breath, all mankind would perish together and man would return to dust."

The Spirit of God is the only thing that keeps us from imploding!

A Jillion Gazillion

In his book, *The Arithmetic of Life and Death,* George Shaffner looks at life through the lens of mathematics. The first chapter calculates the mathematical probability that you would be you. Shaffner calculates the probability that you would get the twenty-three chromosomes you got from your mother as ½ or .5 to the 23rd power—that is 1 in 10 million. The same is true for the twenty-three chromosomes you got from your father. If you multiply the two of them together, you realize that from a biological perspective, the chance that you would be you is 1 in 100 trillion. But you have to factor in that your parents had the same probability, and their parents, and their parent's parents ad infinitum. George Shaffner says the probability that you would be you is a jillion gazillion.

Here is his conclusion, "**Every life is a miracle of immeasurable proportion.**"

Every individual is invaluable and irreplaceable because every individual is absolutely unique. There never has been and never will be anyone like you, but that isn't a testament to you. It's a testament to the God who designed you.

Original
All of us start out as one-of-a-kind originals. Too often we end up carbon copies of someone else. In his essay, *Self-Reliance*, Ralph Waldo Emerson said, **"There is a time in every man's education that he arrives at the conviction that imitation is suicide. He must take himself for better or for worse."**
That is precisely what David did in I Samuel 17:38.
"Then Saul dressed David in his own tunic. He put a coat of armor and on him and a bronze helmet on his head. David fastened on his sword over the tunic and tried walking around, because he was not used to them."
Arming a warrior for battle was a major ritual in David's day. Armor was an extension of the warrior's character. Don't miss the significance of what happens in the locker room. David could have gone into Battle dressed like a king. Saul was offering to outfit him. But David said, "I cannot go in these because I am not used to them. So he took them off."
Counterfactual theory is the branch of history that asks the "what if" questions. Counterfactual theorists are the Monday Morning Quarterbacks of historians. Here's a counterfactual question: what if David had gone out to meet Goliath on Goliath's terms—fully armored, fully armed?
I think David would have lost because David wasn't a swordsman. In fact, he'd probably never touched a sword in his life.
I Samuel 13:19 says, "Not a blacksmith could be found in Israel, because the Philistines said, 'Otherwise the Hebrews will make swords or spears!' So all Israel went down to the Philistines to have their plow-shares, mattocks, axes, and sickles sharpened. On the day of the battle, not a soldier with Saul had a sword or a spear; only Saul and

Jonathan had them."

David wasn't a swordsman. For better or for worse, David was a shepherd. The sword would have posed a greater threat to David, through self-inflicted wounds, than it did to Goliath. But David was deadly with a slingshot. David came to a crossroads. He had a choice to make. He could go into battle as Saul—wear Saul's armor, wield Saul's sword, hold Saul's shield. Or he could go into battle as himself—a shepherd with a slingshot. David decided not to don Saul's armor or brandish Saul's sword for one very good reason. He wasn't Saul.

David decided to be David.

Be Yourself

The sculptor Korczak Ziolkowski invested thirty-six years of his life carving a 563 foot-high statue of Crazy Horse on the granite face of the Yellowstone Mountains—that's eight-feet-higher than the Washington Monument and nine-times-larger than the faces at Mount Rushmore. Following his death in 1982, his children decided to finish the work their father started. Their projected completion date is the year 2050. Why invest a lifetime in one larger-than-life statue? Korczak said, **"When your life is over, the world will ask you only one question: Did you do what you were supposed to do?"**

Why do composers write music? Why do poets pen poetry? Why do artists paint pictures? They do it to give expression to something that is deep within them. That something is their soulprint. They find fulfillment and fruit-fulness—internal satisfaction and external success—because they are doing what they were originally designed and ultimately destined to do. And they know it. The sonata, the poem, and the painting are not just "works of art." They are expressions of the soul. Abraham Maslow said, "A musician must make music, a builder must build, an artist must paint, a poet must write, if he is to be ultimately at peace with himself. What a man can be, he must be."

Significance is one of humankind's deepest-seated needs. We need to be needed. We instinctively ask: what am I here for?

In their book, *Repacking Your Bags*, authors Richard Leider and David Shapiro present research indicating that **the greatest human fear is having lived a meaningless life.** And it's not just our greatest fear. It's our greatest frustration. "There is no agony," says Nora Neale Hurston, "like bearing an untold story inside you."

The failure to give expression to our soulprint—the person God destined us to become—is the taproot of regret. Margaret Culkin Banning said, "Regrets are as personal as fingerprints." Close. Regrets are as personal as soulprints.

"The deepest form of despair," warned Soren Kierkegaard "is to choose to be another than oneself."

At the end of the day, God isn't going to ask, "Why weren't you more like Billy Graham or Mother Teresa?" Or fill in the blank with any other spiritual giant. God is going to ask, "Why weren't you more like you?"

When you try to be who you're not you're second-guessing God.

Shamgar

You need to come to terms with who you're not, but don't let what you can't do keep you from doing what you can!

Here's my personal definition of success: **do the best you can with what you have where you are!**

Don't worry about what you can't do. Do what you can.

You've probably never heard of him before. His name is mentioned in only one verse of Scripture, but that one verse speaks volumes. He is a biblical footnote, but he ranks as one of Israel's most overlooked and underappreciated judges.

Judges 3:31 says, "After Ehud came Shamgar son of

Anath, who struck down six hundred Philistines with an oxgoad. He delivered Israel."

As far as we know, Shamgar had no armor, no military training, and no weapons. All he had was an oxgoad—a long stick used to prod oxen while plowing. When you are choosing weapons to wage war an oxgoad doesn't typically top the list.

Imagine what he could have with a sword or a spear. But he didn't have a sword or a spear! All he had was an oxgoad, and he did the best he could with what he had. Shamgar delivered Israel because he wasn't worried about what he didn't have. He just did the best he could with what he had where he was.

Take a tour de force of the gospels and you'll discover ordinary people who did the best they could with what they had. They are the unsung heroes. All the prostitute had was a bottle of perfume, but she used it to anoint Jesus. All the widow had was two mites, but she gave everything she had. All the boy had was five loaves and two fish, but Jesus used them to feed five thousand.

The prostitute, the widow, and the boy are literally no names. Nowhere in Scripture are their names mentioned. But they are heroes because they did the best they could with what they had where they were. And two thousand years later their stories are read by billions in the best-selling book of all-time. That's what can happen when you simply do the best you can with what you have where you are.

Ectrodactylism

Roger Crawford was born with a rare medical condition called ectrodactylism. It affects only 1 in 90,000 children born in the United States and Roger's condition was worse than most. Roger was born with no hands. Instead of fully-formed hands, thumb-like projections stuck out of both forearms. And Roger was born with severe leg defects. His right foot only had three toes and his left leg was withered so badly that it had to be amputated. The doctors told Roger's parents that he would never walk. His parents didn't believe them.

Roger's parents patiently worked with him and he learned to walk. In fact, he learned to run. His father even encouraged him to play sports. At the age of 12, Roger managed to win a spot as a wide receiver on his school's football team. He didn't get much playing time, but before every game he would dream of scoring a touchdown. One day he got his chance. He ran a long route and caught a pass. The fans erupted. His coaches and teammates were screaming on the sidelines. Roger ran as fast as he could on his artificial leg towards the goal line. He made it all the way to the ten yard line before an opponent caught him and grabbed his left ankle. Roger tried to pull the artificial leg free, but instead the opponent pulled it off. Roger said, "I was still standing up. I didn't know what else to do so I started hopping towards the goal line." He said, "You know, the only thing greater than scoring a touchdown was the look on the face of the kid who was holding my artificial leg."

The baby the doctors said would never walk went on to play collegiate tennis and finished with a 22-11 record. He became the first handicapped person to be certified as a teaching professional by the United States Professional Tennis Association. He now travels across the country telling his story. "The only difference between you and me," he says, "is that you can see my handicap, but I can't see yours. We all have them. When people ask me how I've been able to overcome my physical handicaps, I tell them that I haven't overcome anything. **I've simply learned what I can't do**—such as play the piano or eat with chopsticks—**but more importantly, I've learned what I can do. Then I do what I can do with all my heart and soul.**"

Colossians 3:23 says, "Whatever you do, work at it with

all your heart, as working for the Lord, not for men." *The Message* translates it this way, "Don't just do the minimum that will get you by. Do your best." A literal translation of the original language would read this way: "Whatsoever whatsoever you do, do it heartily heartily as unto the Lord and not unto men."

There is a double emphasis on the two words: whatsoever and heartily. The significance of that is this: Paul is saying it doesn't matter what you do! What matters is that you do the best you can with what you have. The word "heartily" comes from the Greek word *psuche* which is typically translated "life." I think Paul is saying it doesn't matter what you do. **Just do it like your life depended on it.**

Soulprint

⋆⇁═◉═⇀⋆

The genetic uniqueness of every person is evidenced by our unique "prints"—fingerprints, voiceprints, and eyeprints.

John Daugman, a computer scientist at Cambridge University, recently developed the *Iris ID*. The device scans the Iris and stores the image in a computer database. To date, Daugman has stored thirty million images and never encountered two identical irises in his computer cross checks.

In eighty years of fingerprint classification, no two identical prints have ever been found.

"The individual identity of each human person is not only an article of religious faith or an axiom of the Western mind," notes James Hillman in *The Soul's Code*. "Human individuality is also a statistical quasi-certainty."

Our 23 chromosome pairs can line up in 8,388,608 (2^{23}) different ways. Based on potential variability, geneticists postulate the potential existence of as many as seventy trillion genetically unique individuals! But our uniqueness goes way beyond genetics—fingerprints, voiceprints, and eyeprints.

Each of us is born with a unique soulprint—an original design and ultimate destiny.

Psalm 139:14 puts it poetic terms. "Thanks for making me so wonderfully complex! Your workmanship is marvelous." Translation: you are uniquely handcrafted by God himself. Your soulprint has His fingerprints all over it. Ephesians 2:10 says, "We are God's workmanship, created in Christ Jesus to do good works, which God prepared in advance for us to do."

The word "workmanship" comes from the Greek word *poeima*, which can be translated poem, masterpiece, or work of art. You are God's magnum opus.

Vincent Van Gogh said, **"Christ is more of an artist than the artists; he works in the living spirit and the living flesh; he makes men instead of statues."**

Immagine Del Cour

From 1501 to 1504, Michelangelo chipped and chiseled a block of rock that was destined to become history's most famous sculpture. When Michelangelo finished sculpting *David*, he was asked how he could create such a masterpiece from a slab of stone. Michelangelo claimed the masterpiece was already in the rock, he simply removed the excess stone so *David* could escape.

Michelangelo had a phrase for it. As he sculpted *David* he envisioned what he called the *immagine del cour* or heart's image. Michelangelo didn't see a slab of stone. In his mind's eye he saw *David*—the finished product.

All great artists have the same ability. They don't see an empty canvass or slab of stone or blank page. They see the *immagine del cour*—the finished product. And they work backwards.

In the same sense, God works backwards. He knows what he wants us to look like and He's working backwards to help us become who He wants us to be. He is preparing us and perfecting us and positioning us for good works in advance.

Opportunity Knocks

If I had to describe Moses at forty years of age, I'd use the phrase "psyched up." If I had to describe Moses at eighty, I'd use the phrase "psyched out."

At forty, Moses felt like he couldn't do anything wrong. He had a dream of delivering his people, the Israelites, out of slavery. But Moses made a mistake. He took matters into his own hands and killed an Egyptian taskmaster. His feelings were understandable. He was outraged by the vicious mistreatment of his people. But his actions were inexcusable. In God's economy, the means never have and never will justify the ends. **God's will is always accomplished in God's way, with God's power, in God's timing, for God's glory.** No exceptions!

Moses tried to accomplish God's plan in his own way, in his own power, in his own timing and ended up on a "Most Wanted" poster. He fled a fugitive and lived the next forty years tending sheep on the backside of the desert regretting his career-ending, dream-killing miscue. The man who felt like he couldn't do anything wrong at forty, felt like he couldn't do anything right at eighty. His dream of delivering Israel had gathered dust and long since passed the expiration date.

Then God shows up in a burning bush and tells Moses to dust off the dream.

God said to Moses, "I have indeed seen the misery of my people in Egypt. I have heard them crying out because of their slave drivers, and I am concerned about their suffering. So I have come down to rescue them from the hand of the Egyptians and to bring them up out of that land into a good and spacious land, a land flowing with milk and honey so now, go, I am sending you to Pharaoh to bring my people the Israelites out of Egypt."

The burning bush is the place of second chances. One miscue and Moses had been off-stage for forty years. But it's almost as if God says, "Take two. Let's give this another try." The natural window of opportunity had closed. But God opens a supernatural window of opportunity.

The Tide

The English word "opportunity" comes from the Latin phrase *ob portu*. In the days before modern harbors, ships had to wait till flood tide to make it into port. The Latin phrase *ob portu* referred to the moment in time when the tide would turn. The captain and crew would wait for that moment, and knew that if they missed it, they would have to wait for another tide to come in. Shakespeare borrowed the idea in one of his famous verses:

> *There is a tide in the affairs of men*
> *Which, taken at the flood, leads on to fortune*
> *Omitted, all the voyage of their life*
> *Is bound in shallows and in miseries*
> *On such a full sea we are now afloat;*
> *And we must take the current when it serves,*
> *Or lose our ventures*

At forty, Moses tried to accomplish God's plan too soon—before the tide had turned. He became impatient. He got tired of idling in neutral. He wanted to do something, anything to help his people. But he didn't wait for the tide to turn. He acted too soon.

At eighty, he thought it was too late. But in the words of F. Scott Fitzgerald, "**Never confuse a single mistake with a final mistake.**" In other words, don't put a period where God puts a comma! I think Moses had given up on Moses, but God hadn't given up on the Moses!

Wilderness 101

Moses begged God, "Please send someone else to do it."

Moses thought he had been **disqualified**—he had a felony on his record.

I have a friend with a felony on his record. He tells me one of the toughest things about having a felony on your record is getting a second chance. Employers take one look his resume and say, "Thanks, but no thanks." They don't want the inherent risk. Not God! He is an equal-opportunity employer!

God recruits failures like Moses and drafts them in the first round.

I Corinthians 1:26 says, "Think of what you were when you were called. Not many of you were wise by human standards; not many were influential; not many were of noble birth. But God chose the foolish things of the world to shame the wise; God chose the weak things to shame the strong. He chose the lowly things of this world and the despised things—and the things that are not—to nullify the things that are, so that no one may boast before Him."

Moses thought he would live out the rest of his life on the backside of the desert tending sheep, but God had other plans.

Moses thought he was **unqualified**. Forty years earlier he may have submitted his resume, but not now. He said, "O Lord, I have never been eloquent, neither in the past nor since you have spoken to your servant. I am slow of speech and tongue."

What Moses didn't know is that he was uniquely qualified for the job.

God put him through forty years of *Palace 101*. He was the Prince of Egypt. He knew the customs of the Egyptian court. He knew the language. Acts 7:22 says he was "educated in all the learning of the Egyptians."

Then God put him through forty years of *Wilderness 101*. He knew the name of every wild animal. He knew where every watering hole was. He knew the wilderness weather patterns.

You may feel like Moses. Maybe you're on the back side

of the desert because of some mistake you made. You feel disqualified. You feel unqualified. You need to know that God does not call the qualified. **He qualifies the called.** God spent eighty years preparing Moses to deliver Israel and Moses didn't even know it. The most qualified person for the job thought he was disqualified and unqualified. But God was preparing good works in advance. It took eighty years, but Moses was finally ready to do God's will God's way.

Don't forget this simple truth: **everything God allows in your life today is preparation for something He wants to do in your life tomorrow!** Today's problems are preparation for tomorrow's possibilities!

Perfectionist

Lorenzo Ghiberti spent half a century, 1402 to 1452, designing and perfecting the baptistery doors at the Cathedral of Florence. It's no wonder that none other than Michelangelo said they were worthy of being the "gates of paradise."

Fifty years perfecting a set of doors!

Musicians in the world-famous Suzuki program often practice the same note a thousand times every week with one goal in mind—perfect pitch.

An Olympic gymnast will clock 10,000 hours of practice with one goal in mind—a perfect routine.

Artists and athletes are perfectionists. God is no exception.

God will spend a lifetime chipping and chiseling His work of art. He has one goal in mind. He wants to perfect you. Jesus poses what may be the greatest challenge in the gospels in Matthew 5:48. **"Be perfect, therefore, as your heavenly Father is perfect."**

The Greek word for "perfect" is *teleios*. The English word telescope comes from that Greek root. The word looks across time and space and sees who we can and will become. It means **"to complete"** or **"to ripen."** It means **"to fulfill one's intended use."**

One of the last things Jesus said on the cross is recorded in John 19:30. "It is finished." Its three words in English, but its one word in Greek. It is from this root word *teleios* and it means mission accomplished. Jesus was saying, "I did what I came to do."

He fulfilled his purpose.

He was perfection personified.

Pre-Season

After forty years of tending sheep on the backside of the dessert, Moses must have felt like he'd been put out to pasture. I think David felt the same way. His brothers were on the **frontlines** fighting the Philistines while he was stuck on the **sidelines** tending sheep.

What David didn't realize at the time is that preparation for the frontlines usually takes place on the backside of the dessert when no one is watching. God was honing an uncanny ability.

Before his duel with Goliath, David has a flashback. "When a lion or a bear came and carried off a sheep from the flock, I went after it and struck it and rescued the sheep from its mouth. When it turned on me, I seized it by its hair and struck it and killed it."

I have a hunch that David prayed for his sheep. I can't prove it, but I think there are some compelling reasons. What child doesn't pray for their pets? We used to have a bunny named Cottontail that died a couple years ago, but I'm confident we'll meet again in heaven. There is no way that a bunny that was the recipient of that much prayer could be anyplace else! I think David loved and prayed for his sheep just like we love and pray for our pets. Those sheep were his livelihood. Just as farmers pray for a good harvest, a shepherd prays his flock. In fact, I bet David prayed that God would protect his flock by keeping wild animals away.

Evidently those prayers went unanswered because

on numerous occasions, lions and bears attacked David's flock. Maybe David wondered why at the time. He had prayed for protection. Why didn't God answer those prayers? And then it dawns on David as he's sitting in the locker room ready to face Goliath. It all makes sense. It is a eureka moment. David says, "Your servant has killed both lion and bear; this uncircumcised Philistine will be like one of them. The Lord who delivered me from the paw of the bear will deliver me from the hand of this Philistine."

The backside of the dessert was the last place David wanted to be. He wanted to be on the frontlines. But it was on backside of the dessert that God was perfecting the skill that would catapult him into the national limelight. Every time a lion or bear attacked his flock, David pulled a stone out of his shepherd's bag, put it in his slingshot, took aim, and fired. David now realizes that it was target practice. The Bears and Lions were pre-season games. God used them to perfect his skills as a marksman and prepare him for his sudden-death playoff with Goliath (the Giants).

Trash Talk

As David and Goliath come out of the locker room and onto the playing field, Goliath starts talking trash. He curses David, but David is nonplussed.

"You come against me with sword and spear and javelin, but I come against you in the name of the Lord Almighty, the God of the armies of Israel, whom you have defied. This day the Lord will hand you over to me, and I'll strike you down and cut off your head. Today I will give the carcasses of the Philistine army to the birds of the air and beasts of the earth, and the whole world will know that there is a God in Israel."

I love it. No one thinks David has a fighting chance. And David is talking trash!

David slings one stone and scores a KO in the first round.

"So David triumphed over the Philistine with a sling and a stone; without a sword in his hand he struck down the Philistine and killed him."

David wins one of history's greatest upsets, but what you need to understand is this: the battle wasn't won on the frontlines. The battle was won on the backside of the desert! The success that David experienced can be traced back to those pre-season games against the Lions and Bears where God was perfecting David's skills as a marksman.

Maybe you feel like you're on the backside of life. You want to be where the action is, but all you can do is watch. You want that promotion. You want that degree. You're playing the waiting game instead of the dating game. You're on the sidelines when you want to be on the frontlines. What you need to understand is that preparation for the frontlines of life usually happens on the backside of life.

In David's case, God uses this backside experience to hone one skill—slingshot. I don't think David would have ever guessed that that skill would catapult him onto center stage. But God knew.

Maybe there are skills God is developing right now that will serve you and serve Him down the road. Maybe it's an attitude or habit that God is trying to perfect. Maybe it's a character trait—integrity, flexibility, intensity, or humility.

God always begins with the end and works backwards. And he won't stop because He's a perfectionist. He wants to perfect us in every sense of the word.

C.S. Lewis said, "When I invited Jesus in my life, I thought he was going to put up some wallpaper and hang a few pictures. But he started knocking out walls and adding on rooms. I said, 'I was expecting a nice cottage.' But He said, 'I'm making a palace in which to live'."

The Tribe of the Transplanted

Every summer I take a short sabbatical from preaching. Here's why. One of the greatest dangers I face as a pastor is focusing on what God can do through me instead of what God wants to do in me. I feel bad even saying this, but if I'm not careful, my relationship with God can become a means to an end instead of an end in and of itself.

My devotional times can become utilitarian. There is a difference between seeking God to seek God and seeking God because you speak on Sunday! If I cross that line its spiritual manipulation. And God sees right through it. He wants to work through you, but He wants to work in you first. C.S. Lewis said it this way. **"What God does for us he does in us."**

Who you are is more important than what you do because what you do will ultimately be a reflection of who you are.

Lasting change always happens from the inside out. The most important transformation and the deepest transformation and the most difficult transformation is at the level of desire. But anything less is short lived and superficial.

Four Levels

I think there are four levels of transformation.

Level one is **behavioral—it is acting different**. The Pharisees had this level mastered. From a behavioral perspective, they were as good at it gets. But Jesus said, "Their lips honor me, but their hearts are far from me." Behavioral change is good, but it's not good enough. Pavlov could train a dog to make behavioral changes. **Too often we reduce spirituality to a bunch of behaviors and end up with legalism**. God wants the change to go deeper than that.

Level two is **intellectual—it is thinking different**. The word repentance comes from the Greek word *metanoia* which literally means "change of mind." It is a paradigm shift. You think different thoughts. You think deeper thoughts. Intellectual change is good, but it's not good enough. **Too often we reduce spirituality to intellectual assent**. God wants the change to go deeper than that.

Level three is **volitional—it is deciding different**. This is the level where you do what's right even when you feel like doing what's wrong. It is a restructuring of values and making decisions accordingly. Volitional change is good, but it's not good enough. God wants the change to go deeper than that.

Level four is **motivational—it is desiring different**. It goes beyond emotion. It goes beyond passion. It is why we do what we do. **The end goal is genuinely wanting what God wants**. You hate what He hates. You love what He loves. The things that break the heart of God break your heart.

Some of you have never experienced this fourth level of transformation and that's precisely why you're frustrated spiritually. You act different. You think different. You decide different. But you still have those sinful desires that infect everything you do. You do what you don't want to do and don't do what you want to do. It is the spiritual conundrum that Paul describes in Romans 7.

Don't miss this: **no one has behavioral problems. We have desire problems.** We desire the wrong thing too much and the right thing too little.

Galatians 5:24 says, "Those who belong to Christ Jesus have nailed the passions and desires of their sinful nature to His cross and crucified them."

This is half the battle—crucifying sinful desires.

The other half of the battle is allowing God to download new desires.

Psalm 37:4 says, "**Delight yourself in the Lord and he will give you the desires of your heart.**" When we are walking in right relationship with the Lord, God gives us the desires of our hearts. The word "give" means "to conceive." In other words, when we're living for God's glory, God literally downloads new desires!

The Tribe of the Transplanted

Ezekiel 36:25 says, "**I will give you a new heart with new and right desires**, and I will put a new spirit in you. I will take out your stony heart of sin and give you a new obedient heart" (*TNL*).

Our spiritual condition rises or falls on the condition of our heart. If something in your heart is wrong it'll eventually manifest itself and find expression in what you say or what you do. Matthew 12:34 says, "Out of the overflow of your heart the mouth speaks." **No one has behavior problems or attitude problems.** We have heart problems. Bad behaviors and bad attitudes are simply symptoms of heart problems.

I think Richard Foster is right. "Superficiality is the curse of our age." We treat symptoms and ignore causes. **We ask for band aids when what we need is a heart transplant.** In the prophetic words of Jeremiah 8:11, "They offer superficial treatments for my people's mortal wound."

I recently read Charles Siebert's book *A Man After His Own Heart*. He observed a heart transplant at Columbia-Presbyterian in New York City and gives a fascinating play-by-play. It's almost surreal reading about something so medical and so mystical. One surgical team cross-clamped and removed the heart. Another team double-bagged it, put it into a cooler, threw it into the trunk of a car, and drove to where the heart recipient was waiting. The recipient's chest cavity was open and empty. The heart was meticulously grafted and miraculously started beating.

A heart transplant is a marvel of modern medicine, but it goes way beyond what medicine can explain or understand. Medical science is just beginning to rediscover the metaphysical significance of the heart. The heart isn't just a pump. It secretes its own brain like hormones. It has what medical science calls "cellular memory." So a heart transplant isn't just physical. It's metaphysical. A person doesn't just receive a pump. They receive cellular memories.

Siebert attended an annual banquet for transplant recipients and noted their unique appreciation for life. They all spoke in reverent tones about this gift they'd received and their responsibility to honor the donor. They also talked about the new cravings and desires that accompanied the transplant. Siebert concluded, and his research is backed up by numerous studies, that transplant recipients don't just receive a physical organ. They receive "whole new sensory responses, cravings, habits."

Siebert called this group of heart recipients "the tribe of the transplanted."

I can't think of a better description of followers of Christ. We are the tribe of the transplanted. God has given us new hearts with new desires. One byproduct is "whole new sensory responses, cravings, habits."

Acts 13:22 says, "I have found David a man after my own heart."

That's the end goal.

God wants to give us a new heart with new desires. He wants us to want what He wants. And if we want what God wants then everything else takes care of itself!

You begin to think like He thinks and feel what He feels and see what He sees and do what He does. It is living from the inside out. It's no longer about legalism—religion from the outside in. It's no longer about external pressure—caving in to the expectations of others. It is about internal pressure. It is about desire. You desire what is right in God's sight. You want what God wants.

Half-Hearted

One of the reasons I loved Mel Gibson's movie *The Passion* is because it captured what eluded every other movie I've ever seen about Jesus. Most movies about Jesus leave me empty because they don't capture the intensity of Christ. They may accurately depict what he said and did, but not how he said it or how he did it. The missing ingredient is passion.

Jesus wasn't just the wisest or kindest person who ever lived. **Jesus was the most passionate person who ever lived.** He was so passionate that the last twenty-four hours of his life have become known as *The Passion*. He is synonymous with passion.

One of my favorite episodes in the gospels used to raise the most doubt. It didn't fit my flannel-graph caricature of Jesus. Jesus walked into the Temple and turned it upside-down and inside-out. The coolest part is that he made his own whip Indiana-Jones style!

I think the disciples were in a state of shock watching Jesus wield the whip and turn over tables. And then something clicks. They remember something. John 2:17 says, "The disciples remembered that it is written: 'Zeal for your house will consume me'."

Dorothy Sayers said, "**To do them justice, the people**

who crucified Jesus did not do so because he was a bore. Quite the contrary; he was too dynamic to be safe. It has been left for later generations to muffle up that shattering personality and surround him with an atmosphere of tedium. We have declawed the lion of Judah and made him a housecat for pale priests and pious old ladies."

To be like Jesus is to be consumed by zeal.

Here is one of my core convictions: **followers of Christ ought to be the most passionate people on the planet.**

The word enthusiasm comes from two Greek words: *en* and *Theos* or "in God." **The more we get into God the more enthusiastic we become!**

For what it's worth, the fourth Lateran council of 1215 accused the Franciscans of "excessive enthusiasm." I hope you're guilty as charged.

Passion is one thing that sets a relationship with Christ apart from religion. Most world religions are focused on the elimination of desire. The ultimate goal of Buddhism is to exist without desire. I think the goal of a relationship with Christ is the exact opposite. John Eldredge says, "Jesus provokes desire; he awakens it; he heightens it."

C.S. Lewis said that God finds our desires not too strong, but too weak. He said, **"We are half-hearted creatures fooling around with drink and sex and ambition when infinite joy is offered us."**

Half-hearted isn't good enough. Jesus said, "Love the Lord you God with all of your heart and soul and mind and strength."

God doesn't want part of you. He wants all of you. He doesn't want half your brain. He wants your right-brain and left-brain. He doesn't want half your heart. He wants the whole thing!

Half-Alive

C.S. Lewis said we are **half-hearted.**

William James said we are **half-awake**. "Compared with what we ought to be, most of us are only half awake. Our energy is far below the maximum."

I think most of us are **half-present** most of the time. We're not 100% present emotionally or mentally.

And most of us are **half-alive**. Every time we sin or someone sins against us something dies. If you were abused as a child, part of you died emotionally. If your parents divorced at a critical juncture in your life, part of you died relationally. If you struggle with a habitual sin, part of you dies spiritually every time you go down that slippery slope.

None of us is fully alive, but God is in the resurrection business. That's what being "born again" is all about! God resurrects those parts of us that have died. To think of resurrection in purely physical terms is a gross underestimation. God wants to bring you back to life emotionally, relationally, and spiritually.

The prophet Ezekiel visits the valley of dry bones in Ezekiel 37 and the Lord asks a question, "Can these bones live?" Ezekiel says, "You alone know." Then the Lord says to Ezekiel, "Prophesy to these bones and say to them, 'Dry bones, hear the word of the Lord! This is what the Sovereign Lord says to these bones: I will make breath enter you, and you will come to life'."

One of the most beautiful images in *The Chronicles of Narnia* is the breath of Aslan. Aslan's breath has the power to heal or kill or change seasons. He can breathe on things and bring them to life. That is what God does in Genesis 2:7. "The Lord God formed the man from the dust of the ground and breathed into his nostrils the breath of life and man became a living being."

Jewish mystics call it the "cosmic kiss." They refer to the process as *memalleh* or "filling the void." The breath of God is what animates us and sustains us. Without it we'd lose cabin pressure and implode.

For what it's worth, the word Sabbath literally means "to catch one's breath." During the week we are emotionally, physically, and spiritual deflated like a tire with a slow leak. The Sabbath is intended to reinflate our spirits.

Heartfelt Energy

In his book, *High Energy Living*, Dr. Robert Cooper makes a distinction between two kinds of energy: **surface energy** and **heartfelt energy**.

Dr. Cooper says, "People with surface energy may be blessed with Hollywood smiles and schmoozing words, but the energy is self-centered and shallow." Heartfelt energy, on the other hand, is energy that comes from meaning and purpose in life. Dr. Cooper says it is the energy that "awakens and empowers" us. "Without heartfelt energy, life exists **out there**, not **in here**."

One of the most under appreciated qualities of great leaders is their ability to energize others. Great leaders supercharge the people around them with their physical, emotional, mental, and spiritual energy. A great coach energizes his team emotionally. A great professor energizes his class intellectually. A great pastor energizes his congregation spiritually. Leaders are energizers!

Kinetic

When it comes to energy, our 26th president, Theodore Roosevelt was high voltage. If you asked me to describe Roosevelt in one word, it would be "kinetic."

English statesman John Morley likened Roosevelt to Niagara Falls, "Their common quality, which photographs and paintings fail to capture, is a perpetual flow of torrential energy, a sense of motion even in stillness." Roosevelt seemed unstoppable.

On October 14, 1912, Roosevelt was on his way to give a campaign speech in Milwaukee, Wisconsin when a would-be assassin shot him at point-blank range. The .32-caliber bullet lodged two inches deep in his chest. Roosevelt proceeded to get up and deliver his speech. He said, "I don't care a rap about being shot, not a rap." Then, almost in apologetic fashion, he added, "The bullet is in me now, so that I cannot make a very long speech." His speech lasted fifty-three minutes! By the time he finished, he was standing in a pool of his own blood. Not even an assassin's bullet could slow him down.

During his presidency, Roosevelt developed a reputation for eccentric exercises. Senator Henry Cabot Lodge once caught President Roosevelt climbing a tree. He said, "Theodore, if you knew how ridiculous you look up in that tree you'd come down at once." The fact is, Roosevelt didn't care how ridiculous he looked. Climbing a tree paled in comparison with his forays to the Potomac River where he'd go skinny-dipping in the middle of winter—with his cabinet!

On one occasion, White House staff heard loud noises coming from the President's library. It sounded like people were being tossed around the room, and sure enough, they were. Roosevelt was in a tussle with a Japanese Sumo wrestler. Much to the chagrin of Secret Service, Roosevelt even held boxing matches with heavyweight sparring partners.

There was part of Roosevelt that would not be tamed even by the "pomp and circumstance" of the Presidency. Between meetings with heads of state, Roosevelt would sneak upstairs to the attic where his son Quentin had formed the "White House Gang." The President of the United States would chase squealing children until it was time for his next appointment. His romps would leave him so disheveled that he'd have to change clothes before returning to the Oval Office. For better or for worse, Roosevelt was a "Rough Rider."

In *The Rise of Theodore Roosevelt*, Edmund Morris describes Roosevelt's ritual at the end of each day. It typically involved reading a minimum of one book before bed.

He averaged an amazing 500 books per year! After he finished reading, he would brush his teeth, put his revolver beside his pillow, "Then, there be nothing further to do, Theodore Roosevelt will energetically fall asleep."

$E = MC^2$

In John 4, there is a fascinating dialogue between Jesus and his disciples. The disciples were concerned about Jesus because, evidently, he hadn't eaten in quite some time. He was burning the candle at both ends. Crowds that numbered in the thousands constantly swarmed him. The word "crowd" is repeated approximately one hundred times in the gospels.

Imagine the expenditure of energy involved in casting out demons; healing the sick; showing compassion to the outcasts; teaching the crowds; defending his actions to the Pharisees; and adjudicating the disciples' infighting. But even after a full day of ministry, not to mention miles of hiking through mountainous terrain, Jesus would often get up early, stay up late or even pull an all-nighter. Jesus was unstoppable!

How did he keep that pace? Jesus revealed an alternate energy source. "His disciples urged him, 'Rabbi, eat something.' But he said to them, 'I have food to eat you know nothing about.' Then his disciples said to each other, 'Could someone have brought him food?' 'My food,' said Jesus, 'is to the do the will of him who sent me and to finish his work'."

Nothing is as deenergizing as sin—it deflates the spirit. Almost like pulling a plug, sin disconnects us from our supernatural power source. And when you sin, you end up spending energy on things like guilt and shame, fear and anxiety. Frankly, **sin is a waste of energy**. We underestimate the effects of sin not just spiritually, but physically, emotionally and mentally. That's the downside.

Here's the upside. **Nothing is as reenergizing as doing the will of God**—it's like making double-time on a moving sidewalk. It's amazing how far and how fast God can take you when you stay within the guardrails of His "good, pleasing, and perfect will." The Spirit of God energizes you not just spiritually, but physically, emotionally, and intellectually as well.

Heartfelt energy is the byproduct of doing God's will.

Identity Theft

God wants you to become who He created you to be. Satan wants to keep you from becoming who God created you to be. You are the battlefield. War is being waged over the right to your soul. John 10:10 describes the conflict. "The thief comes only to steal and kill and destroy; I have come that they may have life, and have it to the full."

Satan has three primary character traits. He's a tempter and his temptations are always an attempt to get you to settle for less than God's best. He's a deceiver and his deceptions are always an attempt to get you to worship yourself instead of the God who created you. He's an accuser and his accusations are always an attempt to paralyze you by reminding you of what you've done wrong. According to Revelation 12:10, Satan stands before God accusing us night and day. He never stops. He is the quintessential tattle tale.

Zechariah 3 is a record of God's response to Satan's accusations. "Then the angel showed me Jeshua the high priest standing before the angel of the Lord. Satan was there at the angel's right hand, accusing Jeshua of many things. And the Lord said to Satan, 'I, the Lord, **reject your accusations**, Satan. Yes, the Lord, who has chosen Jerusalem, **rebukes you**. This man is like a burning stick that has been snatched from a fire'."

Insert your name into this passage. Now read it again.

God rejects the enemy's accusations against you!

The enemy wants to steal and kill and destroy.

God wants to give you abundant life.

The word "abundant" means "**to superabound in quality and quantity**." God wants to super-size you. He wants to resurrect those parts of you that have died. He wants to set you free so you can become who He created you to be.

Captives

Psalm 139:15 says, "You know me inside and out, you know every bone in my body; You know exactly how I was made, bit by bit, how I was sculpted from nothing into something."

There is a museum in Florence, Italy that contains some of Michelangelo's less famous sculptures. He had intended the sculptures to be used on the tomb of Pope Julius, but he never completed them. The sculptures are partially complete—a hand here, a torso there, a protruding leg, part of a head. None of them are finished. It's almost as if these partial sculptures are trying to break out of the marble—to break free and become what they were intended to be. But they're stuck. Michelangelo called them **captives**.

In his first sermon after going public with his ministry, Jesus said he came to "set the captives free." We tend to think in **forensic terms**—salvation is a "get out of jail free" card. But salvation is so much more than the elimination of sin.

Think of it in **artistic terms**. God is fashioning us and forming us. He is chipping and chiseling. He is setting us free so that we can become who He intended us to be. The word holiness means "wholeness"—God is completing us.

Philippians 1:6 says, "I am confident that He who began a good work will carry it to completion."

We may be half-formed, but God isn't finished with us yet.

Act II: The Process

---

*One's identity is never in one's possession as something
given, completed, and unquestionable.*

Vaclav Havel

In his bestselling book, *Tuesdays with Morrie*, Mitch
Albom reconnects with his college professor, Morrie
Schwartz, and records the lessons he learns about life. On the
seventh Tuesday together they talk about the fear of aging.

Morrie says, "I embrace aging." "It's very simple. As
you grow, you learn more. If you stayed twenty-two, you'd
always be as ignorant as your were at twenty-two."

No offense twenty-two year-olds!

Morrie said, "Aging is not just decay, you know. It's
growth. It's more than the negative that you're going to die,
it's also the positive that you understand you're going to die,
and that you live a better life because of it."

Then Morrie shares a profound perspective on life.
"The truth is, **part of me is every age**. I'm a three-year-
old, I'm a five-year-old, I'm a thirty-seven-year-old, I'm a

fifty-year-old. I've been through all of them, and I know what it's like. I delight in being a child when it's appropriate to be a child. I delight in being a wise old man when it's appropriate to be a wise old man. Think of all I can be! **I am every age, up to my own.**"

The process of self-discovery never ends. I'm not who I was. I'm not who I will become. I am a work in progress. The good news is: **it's never too late to be who you might have been**.

Human Becomings

⊶⟹⟸⊷

Your outlook on life and the outcome of your life will be determined by your answer to two questions. The first and most fundamental question is: **who is God**? The second question is: **who am I**?

According to psychologists, children start developing internal pictures of external realities at about six months of age. The psychological term is **representational intelligence**. A baby develops an internal image of mom at about six months. At about eight months, a baby develops an internal image of dad. Before you know it, your baby will start crawling and walking and they'll develop an internal map of your entire house—especially the location of all staircases and outlets! That process of internalizing external reality never ends. We internalize everything—including God.

Life is an eternal quest to discover who God is. Like a first-generation Polaroid, it literally takes forever for the picture to develop but hopefully the image is getting more and more defined with time. I have a very different picture of who God is now than I did ten years ago. And ten years from now my photo album will look very different. It's not a static thing.

The importance of that internal picture can't be overestimated. A.W. Tozer said, **"What comes to mind when you think about God is the most important thing about you."** How you see God will determine how you see yourself.

So the first question is: who is God? The second question is: who am I? And those questions are not mutually exclusive. They are one and the same quest.

If you want to get to know who you are, you need to get to know who God is. The medieval mystic, Saint Teresa of Avila, said, **"As I see it, we shall never succeed in knowing ourselves unless we seek to know God."**

The more you get to know God the more you get to know yourself because God knows you better than you know you. That is the embedded logic in Psalm 139:1-4. "O Lord, you have searched me and you know me. You know when I sit and when I rise; you perceive my thoughts from afar. You discern my going out and my lying down; you are familiar with all my ways. Before a word is on my tongue you know it completely, O Lord."

There are lots of people who "know" me. They recognize my face or know my name. But they don't know me like my friends know me. My friends know my hobbies and hangups, but my friends don't know me the way my family knows me. My family sees an unguarded side of me that I don't expose to the rest of the world, but my family doesn't know me like my wife knows me. After twelve years of marriage we can communicate via mental telepathy, but even my wife doesn't know me like I know me. I'm with me all the time! Now let me bring this full-circle. I know myself pretty well, but even I don't know me the way God knows me!

There is nothing about you that God doesn't know. He knows the deepest hurts and highest hopes that you've never verbalized. He knows every engram—the memory traces that record every experience on the cerebral cortex of your brain. He hears every sigh—those low-frequency distress signals you can't put into words. He knows the number of hairs on your head. God knows you better than you know you. So if you want to get to know yourself you better get to know God.

Sandor McNab says, "**Nothing determines who we will become so much as those things we choose to ignore.**" You can choose to ignore God. But you'll always be a stranger to yourself. The reason is simple: God knows more about you than you know about you! You are designed and destined by God.

You'll never find yourself if you're looking for yourself. C.S. Lewis said the first step in finding yourself is forgetting about yourself altogether. "Your real, new self will not come as long as you are looking for it. It will come when you are looking for Him." Lewis said, "Look for yourself, and you will find in the long run only hatred, loneliness, despair, rage, ruin, and decay. But look for Christ and you will find Him, and with Him everything else thrown in."

Gofer

David asks the age-old question in II Samuel 7:18. "Then King David went in and sat before the Lord and prayed, 'Who am I, O Sovereign Lord, and what is my family that you have brought me this far'?"

The answer to that question depends upon whom you ask.

Ask David's father, Jesse, and he'd say David was a shepherd. You remember the story. Samuel the prophet shows up in Bethlehem to anoint the next king of Israel. He tells Jesse, David's father, to gather his sons so that one of them can be anointed king. Jesse doesn't even bother to call David. His own dad didn't see who David could and would become. When Samuel asks, "Are these all the sons you have," Jesse says, almost as an afterthought, "There is still the youngest, but he is tending the sheep." When Jesse looked at David he saw a shepherd—no more, no less.

Ask his brothers, and they'd say David was a gofer. He was their errand boy carrying brown bag lunches to the frontlines. One day he showed up at their tent and started asking about Goliath. His brother puts him in his place. "When Eliab, David's oldest brother heard him speaking with the men, he burned with anger at him and asked, 'Why have you come down here? And with whom did you leave those few sheep in the desert? I know how conceited you are and how wicked your heart is; you came down only to watch the battle'." Ouch! David offers the typical little brother response, "Now what have I done?" This wasn't a one-time incident. David was the runt of the litter and his brothers treated him that way—no more, no less.

Ask Saul and he'd say David was a boy amongst men. When David volunteered to fight Goliath he said, "You are not able to go out against this Philistine and fight him; you are only a boy, and he has been a fighting man from his youth."

I don't think anyone saw anything special in David, but he's in good company. Some of the most successful figures in history seemed less than ordinary, anything but special.

Beethoven's teacher called him "hopeless as a composer." Edison's teacher called him "stupid." Walt Disney was fired from his first job for his "lack of ideas." Einstein's teacher said he was "mentally slow." The NY Times said Robert Goddard, the father of modern rocketry "lacked the common sense ladled out in high school" because he dreamed of shooting a rocket to the moon. In 1954, Jimmy Denny, manager of the Grand Old Opry, fired Elvis Presley after one performance. He told the future King of Rock-n-Roll, "You ain't goin' nowhere son. You ought to go back to drivin' a truck."

Maybe you've gotten some negative assessments on a report card or annual review. Like David, you have a choice.

You can listen to the negative assessments or you can listen to God. **Who you listen to will determine who you become.**

If David had accepted their assessment of him he would have never challenged Goliath or written the Psalms or become King of Israel. David would have continued herding sheep and running errands. But he refused to accept their assessment of him for one simple reason. He never asked them, "Who am I?" He asked God!

David's father saw a shepherd. His brothers saw a gofer. Saul saw a boy. But God saw a king!

If you want an accurate assessment of who you are, ask God the question, "Who am I?"

Human Becomings

In his letter *De Profundis*, Oscar Wilde said, "The final mystery is oneself. When one has weighed the sun in the balance, and measured the steps of the moon, and mapped out the seven heavens star by star, there still remains oneself. Who can calculate the orbit of his own soul?"

Life is a process of self-discovery. We aren't human beings. We are human becomings. I'm not who I was. And I'm not who I will be.

Fredrick Buechner described the process in his book *The Alphabet of Grace*. **"Beneath the face I am a family plot. All the people I have ever been are buried there—** the bouncing boy, his mother's pride; the pimply boy and secret sensualist; the reluctant infantryman; the beholder at dawn through hospital plate-glass of his first-born child. All these selves I was I am no longer, not even the bodies they wore are my body any longer, and although when I try, I can remember scraps and pieces about them, I can no longer remember what it felt like to live in side their skin. Yet they live inside my skin to this day, they are buried in me somewhere, ghosts that certain songs, tastes, smells, sights, tricks of weather can raise, and although I am not the same as they,

I am not different either because their having been then is responsible for my being now. I am like a candle lit from a candle lit from a candle, as Gautama said, the traveling flame never the same and never different either. **And buried in me too are all the people I have not been yet but might be someday.**"

"Becoming a person," observed Rollo May in *Man's Search for Meaning*, "involves going through several stages of consciousness of one's self." Even Jesus went through the process. He had a profound sense of identity and destiny at twelve years of age. He said, "I have to be about my Father's business." But Jesus had to learn reading, writing, and arithmetic like the rest of us!

Reggie McNeal writes, "Jesus was fully human. This means that he went through life development stages, including a growing awareness of who he was and what he came to do. To grow up without having to struggle with basic identity issues would make him less than human."

Connect the Dots

Looking back on life is like a game of connect the dots. Only in the game of life, the dots are unnumbered. And in the words of Anne Porter, "The past is never where you think you left it."

Each life is full of dots—defining moments. Those defining moments are a sneak preview of one's destiny. **"There is always one moment in childhood,"** says Graham Greene, **"When the door opens and lets the future in."**

What golf fan hasn't seen the home video of three-year-old Tiger Woods swinging a child-sized golf club? That home video was a sneak preview of Tiger's destiny.

Many stars of the silver screen made their Hollywood debut as childhood prodigies—Ron Howard, Jodie Foster, Judy Garland. The famous filmmaker, Ingmar Bergman, went to the cinema for the first time when he was seven years old. "I was overcome with a fever that has never left me," Bergman later reflected. "Sixty years have gone by and nothing has changed; the fever is the same."

When Wolfgang Amadeus Mozart was a young boy, he visited the Sistine Chapel in Rome and was entranced by a piece of music titled *the Miserere* by Gregorio Allegri. Mozart wanted a copy of the music, but the Sistine Chapel would not allow that particular musical score to be copied under any circumstances. It could only be performed inside the Sistine Chapel. Mozart attended one more performance of *the Miserere*, went home, and wrote out the entire musical score from memory!

At twelve years of age, Jesus astounded the teachers of the law with his understanding of the law. That episode was a sneak preview. I wonder if any of those teachers remembered him eighteen years later when his public ministry began.

Every life is full of dots—defining moments that change the trajectory of one's life forever. For some, those dots are obvious and unmistakable. For others, they are obscure and almost imperceptible.

"Many lives have a mystical sense," observed Alexander Solzhenitzyn. "But not everyone reads it aright. More often than not it is given to us in cryptic form, and when we fail to decipher it, we despair because our lives seem meaningless. The secret of a great life is often a man's success in deciphering the mysterious symbols vouchsafed to him, understanding them and so learning to walk in the true path."

Triumphal Procession

One of my heroes is Corrie Ten Boom. During the Nazi occupation of Holland, the Ten Boom family hid Jews in their house. Their home was raided on February 28, 1944, and Corrie was sent to a concentration camp. Though an amazing series of circumstances she survived and her story was made into a movie called *The Hiding Place*. I saw the movie when I was five years-old and afterwards I asked Jesus into my heart.

When Corrie Ten Boom spoke to audiences about her experiences she would often keep her head down. It looked like she was reading her notes, but she was actually working on a piece of needlepoint. After telling her story of the cruelty in the camps and the death of her father and sister and her miraculous release she would hold up the backside of the needlepoint. It was just a jumble of colors and threads with no discernible pattern. She'd say that's how we see our lives—sometimes it makes no sense. Then she'd turn the needlepoint over to reveal the finished side. Corrie would conclude by saying, "This is how God views your life and someday we will have the privilege of viewing it from His point of view."

Corrie could have questioned why she had to suffer in a Nazi concentration camp. It didn't make sense. It was unfair. But somehow God used the suffering of a woman named Corrie Ten Boom living in Holland in 1944 to lead a five year-old boy named Mark Batterson living in Minneapolis, Minnesota in 1975 to Christ.

II Corinthians 2:14 says, "Thanks be to the God who always leads us in triumphal procession in Christ."

Let God Engineer

I appreciate the brutal honesty of John Eldredge in his book, *Waking the Dead*. "Twenty clear days a year—that sounds about like my life. I think I see what's really going on about that often. The rest of the time, it feels like fog, like the bathroom mirror after a hot shower. I'd love to wake up each morning knowing exactly who I am and where God is taking me. Zeroed in on all my relationships, undaunted in my calling. It's awesome when I do see. But for most of us, life seems more like driving along with a dirty windshield and then turning into the sun."

Oswald Chambers said the same thing in different words. **"I never see my way. I never have far-seeing plans."** I can't tell you how comforting that was when I first read it. I'd love to have the twenty-five year plan, but I've found that God typically leads me one step at a time. It forces me to live in constant reliance upon him and sensitivity to His spirit. I just need to keep putting one foot in front the other!

I've always admired **plotters**—people who see into the future. I want to be a visionary who sees the future. But I've come to admire **plodders**—people who keep putting one foot in front of the next through the tough times. You can knock them down, but they get back up and keep moving forward. And what gets them back up is that sense of destiny.

Oswald Chamber's motto was **"let God engineer."** That is what a sense of destiny is all about. It is this unshakable conviction that even in the most confusing and frustrating of circumstances God is working His plan in your life.

Explanatory Style

Joseph endured a seventeen year string of "bad luck." Things went from bad to worse. His brothers faked his death. He was sold into slavery. He was falsely accused and convicted of rape. He was left to languish in an Egyptian dungeon.

Then, in what may be the most precipitous rise to political power in history, Joseph became Prime Minister of Egypt overnight.

Joseph looks back over his life in Genesis 50:20 and says to the brothers who betrayed him. **"You intended to harm, but God intended it for good to accomplish what is now being done, the saving of many lives."**

In his book *Learned Optimism*, Dr. Martin Seligman says that all of us have what he calls an "explanatory style" to account for life's experiences. He says, **"Explanatory style is the manner in which you habitually explain to**

yourself why events happen."
Let me give you an example.
You're at a restaurant waiting for your date. You were supposed to meet at seven o'clock, but forty-five minutes later your date is a no show. At some point, you need to explain the absence so you develop mental scenarios of why they aren't there.
You could think, "He stood me up," causing you to become mad. You could jump to conclusions, "She doesn't love me anymore," causing you to become sad. You might think, "He was in an accident," causing you to feel anxious. You could think, "She's working overtime so that she can pay for our meal," causing you to feel grateful. Naïve, but grateful. You might think, "He's with another woman," causing you to feel jealous. Or you could think, "This gives me a perfect excuse to break up with her," which causes you to feel relieved.
Same situation. Very different explanations!
The significance of that is this: **there are lots of different explanations for every experience.** You can't control your experiences, but you can control your explanations. And your explanations are more important than your experiences! Dr. Seligman says, "Your way of explaining events to yourself determines how helpless you become, or how energized, when you encounter everyday setbacks as well as momentous defeats."
If anybody could have developed a martyr mentality it was Joseph. Joseph could have come up with any number of explanations. "God has forsaken me." "God is angry with me." "God has forgotten me." "God has given up on me." "God doesn't exist." But Joseph's explanation is Genesis 50:20. "You intended to harm me, but God intended it for good to accomplish what is now being done, the saving of many lives."
That one verse summarizes him outlook on life. It was

his explanatory style. He looks back over his life—all the dysfunction and betrayal and confusion and injustice and prejudice and pain—and he sees the hand of God. There is a rhyme and a reason for everything that happens. Joseph never lost his sense of destiny.

Do or Die

I think there is a "do or die" moment for every dream. Something has to die for the God-given dream to stay alive.

I recently met a pastor who gave up 16,000 shares and a $160,000 salary with *Microsoft* a decade ago to plant a church making $26,000. In the eyes of his employer he was committing occupational suicide. He asked God to give him one person for every share he gave up! The church he started is well on the way averaging more than 4,000 people in weekend attendance! **The more you are willing to give up the more God can use you.** And if you're willing to give up everything there is nothing God can't do!

Abraham's do or die moment came at Mount Moriah. He raised the knife to sacrifice His son, but God provided a ram in the thicket. Esther's do or die moment came in the King's court when she jeopardized her own life to save the life of her people. Nehemiah put his career on the line in Nehemiah 2:5 when he told King Artaxerxes about his dream to rebuild the wall of Jerusalem. He passed the point of no return. It was do or die.

My "do or die" moment came in college. At the end of my freshman year I realized I had never asked God what he wanted me to do with my life. So I asked Him. That began a six-month process of seeking God for direction. That process culminated for me in August of 1989. Our family was on vacation at Lake Ida in Alexandria, Minnesota. I got up early one morning and did a prayer walk down some dirt roads and took a shortcut through a cow pasture. In the middle of that cow pasture I heard what I've come to call the inaudible yet unmistakable voice of God. I knew that God was calling me into full-time ministry.

To make a long story short, I gave up a full-ride scholarship at the University of Chicago to transfer to Central Bible College. The University of Chicago was one of the top-ranked universities in the country academically. Lots of people told me I was committing **academic suicide**. But my full-ride scholarship at the University of Chicago had to die for me to pursue my God-given calling.

Did I ever have second thoughts? Absolutely! But here is what I know for sure: I would have never been ready to plant a church at twenty-six if I hadn't made the move. Everything in my life traces back to that one choice that changed the trajectory of my life.

D²: Dual-Destiny

⊷═◉═⊷

All of us have a dual-destiny (D²). One destiny is universal—to be conformed to the image of Christ. The other destiny is **unique**—to fulfill God's unique plan for your life.

Humankind was created in the image of God. Like a time-worn picture, the image is stained by sin. But God reversed the effects of sin on the cross. The word "convert" means "to reverse." **God does reverse-engineering.** He restores the original image.

II Corinthians 3:18 describes the process in time-lapse fashion. "We, who with unveiled faces all reflect the Lord's glory, are being transformed into His likeness, with ever-increasing glory, which comes from the Lord."

Albedo is a measurement of how much light a celestial body reflects. The planet Neptune, for example, has an albedo of .84—84% of the light that hits Neptune is reflected. Our night-light, the moon, has an albedo of .07—it only reflects 7% of the light that hits it.

The end result of this lifelong process of transformation is a spiritual albedo of 1 or 100% reflectivity of God's glory. We reflect his love and beauty and glory. People look at us and see Jesus. We become a mirror image of Christ.

Hero Worship

Several centuries ago, Thomas Carlyle wrote a book titled *On Heroes, Hero-Worship, and the Heroic in History.* He said, "**Hero-worship exists for ever, everywhere.**" It is the taproot of the human spirit. We need someone to look up to, someone to pattern our lives after, someone to become like. Carlyle said hero worship is the "germ" and "highest instance" of Christianity.

I think Jesus needs to be accepted not just as Lord and Savior. I think He must be accepted as hero—the one we aspire to be like. Jesus was hero to his disciples. They lived in jaw-dropping awe at the things he said and did.

As a kid I had my share of heroes. Most of them were athletes because I loved sports. I loved watching Walter Payton play football. He was the perfect combination of grace and power. I remember so many plays when sweetness was trapped behind the line of scrimmage and somehow he would dance through the defense and turn a five-yard loss into a five-yard gain. Payton's trademark was the "up and over" at the goal line. He would take a handoff behind the line of scrimmage, fly up and over the offensive and defensive lineman, and land in the end zone for a touchdown.

I still remember piling up pillows in our basement and pretending to be Walter Payton. Hour after hour we would jump over those pillows and score imaginary touchdowns. When it came to football I wanted to be like sweetness.

In Junior High, I had another hero. Like every other kid living in the Chicago area in 1984, I become a Michael Jordan fan. Almost every game he would have some spectacular move and I'd go out in my driveway and try to duplicate it. I couldn't jump as high as "Air Jordan" so sometimes I'd pull out a trampoline and use it as a springboard to imitate his dunks. When it came to basketball I wanted to be like Mike.

I wanted to play football like Payton. I wanted to play basketball like Jordan.

In the same sense, I want to play the game life like Jesus!

If I had to summarize my life goal in one sentence this would be it: **I want to know Jesus more and be more like Him.** He is my hero. I want to think like he thought. I want to pray like He prayed. I want to live like he lived.

In a sense, **discipleship is hero worship**.

Rick Warren says, "Everybody eventually surrenders to someone or something. If not to God, you will surrender to the opinions of others, to money, to resentment, to fear, or to your own pride, lusts, or ego. You were designed to worship God—and if you fail to worship him, you will create other things (idols) to give your life to."

All of us pattern our lives after someone. Psychologists call it "the chameleon effect." Followers of Christ simply make a conscious and conscientious decision to imitate Christ. Jesus isn't just Lord and Savior. He's hero. And we follow in His footsteps.

Thomas Carlyle said, "Christianity is the highest instance of hero worship."

Our universal destiny is Christlikeness.

Conformity

One of our core values at National Community Church is **maturity doesn't equal conformity**. That doesn't mean that we want to be different for difference sake, but what some churches call spiritual maturity is nothing more than cultural conformity. People dress the same way and talk the same way and act the same way and that's the measuring stick of maturity. But that's not spirituality. That's superficiality. Too many churches and too many Christians settle for conformity instead of striving for maturity. Maturity results in diversity—different people with different personalities using different gifts in different ways!

We need to worry a lot less about conforming to the people around us. And we need to worry a lot more about conforming to Christ. And Jesus was a nonconformist! That's why he was crucified. He didn't fit into the religious leaders' "religious box." He was counterintuitive and countercultural, anything but a conformist.

Francis Schaeffer said, "One of the greatest injustices we do to our young people is to ask them to be conservative. Christianity is not conservative, but revolutionary. To be conservative today is to miss the whole point, for conservatism means standing in the flow of the status quo, and the status quo no longer belongs to us. If we want to be fair, we must teach the young to be revolutionaries, revolutionaries against the status quo."

Carpe Diem

In the movie *Dead Poet's Society*, Professor Keating, played by Robin Williams, walks to the beat of a different drummer. He has the daunting task of teaching poetry to teenage boys in a private school, but Professor Keating has a gift. He makes the poetry come alive. In one scene, the class is huddled in front of a trophy case with yellowed pictures of a bygone football team. One of the students, Mr. Pitt, reads a page of poetry,

> *Gather ye rosebuds while you may*
> *Old time is still a-flying.*
> *And this same flower that smiles today*
> *Tomorrow will be dying.*

Professor Keating explains, "The Latin term for this sentiment is carpe diem." He asks for a translation and gets one, "Carpe diem, seize the day."

As the class leans in for a closer look at the faded

photographs in the trophy case, Professor Keating whispers, "Car-pe...car-pe...carpe diem. Make your lives extraordinary."

Colossians 4:5 says, "Make the most of every opportunity." That phrase "make the most" in Colossians 4:5 is translated "redeem" in the *KJV*. It comes from the Greek word *exagorazo*, which means, "to rescue from loss." In other words, seize the day!

In his best-selling book, *What Color is Your Parachute?*, author Richard Bolles says, "The story in the Gospels of Jesus going up on the mount and being transfigured before the disciples is to me a picture of what calling is all about: **taking mundane tasks and figuring out how to transfigure them.**"

That's the message of I Corinthians 10:31 in a nutshell. "So whether you eat or drink or whatever you do, do it all to the glory of God." What could be more mundane than eating and drinking? But that's the point: even the most mundane tasks can be transfigured into an act of worship!

Oswald Chambers said, "**It is inbred in us that we have to do exceptional things for God: but we have not. We have to be exceptional in the ordinary things.**"

Opportunity Costs

Jeremiah 46:17 is one of the saddest epitaphs in Scripture. "Give Pharaoh of Egypt the title King of Bombast, **the man who missed his moment.**"

Howard Schultz, CEO of *Starbucks*, reflects on what he calls his "opportunity of a lifetime" in his autobiography *Pour Your Heart into It*. "This is my moment, I thought. **If I don't seize the opportunity**, if I don't step out of my comfort zone and risk it all, if I let too much time tick on, **my moment will pass.** I knew that if I didn't take advantage of this opportunity, I would replay it in my mind for my whole life, wondering: what if?"

Howard Schultz's date with destiny was August 15, 1987. He described his opportunity as a case of the "salmon swallowing the whale," but he purchased Starbucks for $4 million. On June 26, 1992, less than five years after making the most of this opportunity, Starbucks' stock went public. It was the second most active stock traded on the NASDAQ and by the closing bell, its market capitalization stood at $273 million!

Life is an endless string of opportunities. It's our ability or inability to see and seize those opportunities that will make us or break us. We'll regret the ones we missed and rejoice over the ones we seized.

Date with Destiny

On October 31, 1517, a little-known Monk named Martin Luther walked up to the Castle Church in Wittenberg, Germany. In those days, church doors served as a community bulletin board. He posted a piece of paper on the door attacking the practice of indulgences that had crept into the church. Forgiveness was no longer a free gift to be received, but something to be purchased. Martin Luther paid a price. He was excommunicated from the church. But that one act of courage sparked the protestant reformation.

October 31, 1517 was Martin Luther's date with destiny.

On May 10, 1940, Winston Churchill was asked by King George VI to lead Britain against the forces of Nazism. At the time, England was on the losing side. It seemed like an impossible undertaking. But Churchill later recounted, **"I felt as if I were walking with destiny, and that all my past life had been but a preparation for this hour and for this trial."**

May 10, 1940 was Churchill's date with destiny.

On December 1, 1951, Rosa Parks was tired from a long day at work. She got onto a bus in Montgomery, Alabama. Little did she know that this bus ride would forever change her life and the course of history in America. Segregation laws required black passengers to give up their seat for white passengers. Rosa Parks refused to do it and she paid a price. She was arrested and lost her job. But that one act of courage had a domino effect. It inspired a citywide boycott of the bus system in Montgomery, and it sparked a court battle. Within two years, bus segregation was ruled unconstitutional.

In her book, *Quiet Strength*, Rosa Parks said, **"Our mistreatment was not right, and I was just tired of it. I knew there was a possibility of being mistreated, but an opportunity was being given to me."**

December 1, 1955 was Rosa Park's date with destiny.

On March 13, 474 BC, King Xerxes ordered the execution of every Jew in all 127 provinces of the Persian Empire. The Jewish people were given less than a year to live. But in the words of Mordecai, "Who knows but that you have come to royal position for such a time as this?"

March 13, 474 BC was Esther's date with destiny.

Checkmate

In the early 1990's, chess master, Bobby Fisher, won $1 million in a chess match in Croatia. On the way back to America he stopped at the *Louvre* in Paris to see the famous painting *Checkmate*.

The painting depicts a chess match in progress. On one side of the chessboard is a young man with a panicked expression on his face, sweat droplets beginning to run down his face. Seated across the chessboard is Satan. He has a chess piece in his hand and about to make his move. As the name of the painting suggests, the young man is trapped—Satan has him in check.

Bobby Fisher requested that a chessboard be set up and he put all the chess pieces on the chessboard just as they were pictured in the painting. He played Satan's last move and then studied the board for quite a while looking for possible countermoves. He finally broke his studied silence. "Don't worry, young man, you've got another move." He proceeded to make a countermove that didn't just get the young man out of check, but left Satan in checkmate!

The book of Esther is a like a cosmic chess match between God and Satan. Satan positions his pawn, Haman, in a strategic cabinet position in Xerxes administration. He drafts an executive order calling for the genocide of the Jews. And Satan says "check." Game over. It seems like an impossible situation. Xerxes used his signet ring to sign, seal, and deliver the execution order. It was irreversible. But God comes up with a brilliant countermove. I love the way Esther 9:1 puts it. "The tables were turned and the Jews got the upper hand." God strategically positions his pawns, Esther and Mordecai, as Queen and Prime Minister of Persia, and says "checkmate."

GPS

Right now, Global Positioning System (GPS) Satellites are orbiting the earth broadcasting signals that enable jetliners, ocean liners, cruise missiles, and hikers with handheld GPS receivers to know their exact latitude and longitude at any time.

A few years ago we adopted an eight-month old Pug named Stanley. Stanley looked like a normal dog. Well, maybe less than normal. Pugs look like they ran full-speed, face-first into a parked car. Stanley acted like a normal dog. He chased parked cars. He barked at dogs that were bigger than him. And he periodically left "housewarming" gifts if we don't let him outside often enough.

Stanley looked normal and acted normal, but we affectionately referred to Stanley as "Microdog" because a microchip was inserted under his skin when he was a puppy. The chip was so small that it fit in a hypodermic needle and the vet injected the microchip under his skin where it will remain for life. For a $15 fee paid to *PETrac*, Stanley will never get lost. At the time, we weren't sure whether that was a good thing or bad thing but *PETrac* sent me on a guilt trip with one of their flyers. "Every two seconds a family pet is lost. Now you can easily protect Your Loved One! Affordable lifetime protection—it's only $15.00. By enrolling in *PETrac*, you distinguish your pet as a special member of your family." In other words, if you don't get a microchip installed in your dog, you don't really love your dog!

If you are a follower of Christ, you may look normal and you may act normal, but you aren't. You are part of God's global positioning system (GPS). God is in the business of strategically positioning us in the right place at the right time.

Sovereign Insomnia

The book of Esther is unique because it's the only book in the Bible where the name of God is not mentioned! He is invisible, but his fingerprints are everywhere.

Esther 2:21 says, "During the time Mordecai was sitting at the king's gate, Bigthana and Teresh, two of the king's officers who guarded the doorway, became angry and conspired to assassinate King Xerxes. But Mordecai found out about the plot and told Queen Esther, who in turn reported it to the king, giving credit to Mordecai. And when the report was investigated and found to be true, the two officials were hanged on a gallows. All this was recorded in *The Book of the Annals* in the presence of the king."

Mordecai was in the right place at the right time—he overheard and uncovered an assassination plot. He wasn't rewarded, but that was part of God's plan. Mordecai's good deed was recorded in *The Book of the Annals*.

Fast-forward five years.

Haman, the Prime Minister of Persia, had a vendetta against Mordecai. He had a breakfast appointment with Xerxes where he planned to ask permission to execute Mordecai. The night before, Xerxes experienced a case of

sovereign insomnia. Then, out of all the books in his library, he asked for *The Book of the Annals*. And it fell open to the story of Mordecai's heroics.

When Mordecai wasn't rewarded for uncovering the assassination plot, I wonder if he felt overlooked and unappreciated. Was he bitter about not getting a reward? Like a fine wine that gets better with the passage of time, **sometimes God's delayed blessings are his best blessings**. When his blessings are delayed, hold onto his promises! Nothing goes unrewarded. You can bank on Matthew 6:4. "Your Father, who sees what is done in secret, will reward you."

To make a long story short, Haman walked in for his breakfast appointment and King Xerxes said, "What should be done for the man the king delights to honor?" Haman naturally thought King Xerxes was talking about him so he answered the king, "For the man the king delights to honor, have them bring in a royal robe the king has worn and a horse the king has ridden, one with a royal crest place on its head. Then let the robe and the horse be entrusted to one of the king's most noble princes. Let them robe the man and the king delights to honor and lead him on the horse through the city streets, proclaiming before him, 'This is what is done for the man the king delights to honor'."

Then Haman gets the shock of his life. King Xerxes says, "Go, at once, get the robe and the horse and do just as you have suggested for Mordecai the Jew, who sits at the king's gate." That was Haman's first clue that is was going to be a bad day!

Five years had come and gone with no reward. But God saves his blessings for the right time and the right place. You couldn't write the script any better than this! God's timing is impeccable. He's never early. He's never late. He's always right on time!

In A Pit With A Lion On
A Snowy Day

❖⟫═◉═⟪❖

I'll never forget January 29, 1995. I was a guest speaker at a church in Washington, DC that Sunday morning. After I finished preaching, the pastor closed the service in prayer. It started out as a generic benediction, then he turned toward my wife (yes, I was peeking) and prayed, "God, bless the little one within." After praying, he explained that God had given him a word of prophecy that Lora was pregnant with our first child. The doctor confirmed the prophecy the next week and as far as I know, we are the only couple I've ever heard of that found out they were pregnant in church! That prophecy became reality on September 26, 1995, the day our son, Parker, was born.

Before Lora and I knew about Parker, God knew about Parker. Parker was God's idea to begin with. The word "predestined" took on a whole new meaning for me. From day one, we knew that God had a special plan and purpose for Parker's life. He was no accident. Psalm 139:16 says it this way. **"All the days ordained for me were written in your book before one of them came to be."**

In his book, *The Purpose-Driven Life*, Rick Warren says, "While there are illegitimate parents, there are no illegitimate children. Many children are unplanned by their parents, but they are not unplanned by God."

God was thinking about you long before you were thinking about him. Long before you were conceived by your parents, you were conceived in the mind of God. God had a plan and purpose for your life before you were born, before your parents were born, before the universe itself was born.

The Road Ahead

Ephesians 2:10 says, "We are God's workmanship, **created in Christ Jesus to do good works prepared in advance.**"

The word "prepared" is drawn from the ancient custom of sending servants ahead of a King to secure safe passage. God turns the tables. The King of Kings goes in advance of His servants and prepares the road ahead. Maybe the best way of saying it is this: **God is in the business of strategically positioning us in the right place at the right time.** And that ought to give us a sense of destiny.

Let me put some skin on it.

A few years ago I took my son, Parker, fishing for the first time at the Tidal Basin in the shadow of the Jefferson Memorial. He knew nothing about fishing so I basically did everything for him. I put the leader on the line. I put the hook on the leader. And I put the worm on the hook. I did the casting and reeling. I watched the bobber. And when the bobber finally went under I hooked the fish. I reeled the fish in until it was right offshore. I did everything. I engineered that experience. Then, like any good dad, I handed the pole to my son and grabbed my camcorder so I could catch him catching "his" first fish!

That is how God works in our lives. He is setting you up! He is around every corner preparing good works for us in advance. The theological word is providence.

I have a friend who used to work as a Special Agent in White House Communications. Before the President traveled anywhere, an advance team from White House Communications would make preparations. They would ship several planeloads of supplies and equipment. They set up phone wires and security systems. They cased the place to ensure the safety of the President. They helped plan the itinerary—what time the president would arrive, by what route, how he would be escorted into and out of the event. They left no stone unturned. Everything was "prepared in advance." All the president had to do was show up!

God is preparing the road ahead. All we have to do is show up!

Bad Luck

II Samuel 23 tells the story of one of David's mighty men. "Benaiah was a valiant fighter from Kabzeel, who performed great exploits. He struck down two of Moab's best men. **He went down into a pit on a snowy day and killed a lion.** And he struck down a huge Egyptian. Although the Egyptian had a spear in his hand, Benaiah went against him with a club. He snatched the spear from the Egyptian's hand and killed him with his own spear."

If you're in a pit with a lion on a snowy day you've got serious problems! That qualifies as a bad day! Some might call it bad luck. Not only was he in a pit. He was in a pit with a lion. And it was snowing which means this cat was hungry and it was slippery. Hold that thought.

II Samuel 23:22 says, "And David appointed him as chief over his bodyguard."

Getting stuck in a pit with a lion on a snowy day is the last place any of us would want to be, but you've got to admit that "I killed a lion in a pit on a snowy day" looks pretty good on your resume if you're applying for a bodyguard position.

I can picture David flipping through a stack of resumes. "I majored in security at the University of Jerusalem." "I did an internship with the Palace Guard." "I worked for Brinks Armored Chariots." Those aren't bad credentials, but David comes to the next resume in the stack. It says, "I killed a lion in a pit on a snowy day."

David must have said, "When can you start?" That is the kind of guy you want in charge of your bodyguard. Can you see how God used his "bad luck" to build his resume and set him up for his first big break?

Benaiah climbed all the way up the military chain-of-command to become Commander-in-Chief of David's army. But it all started on a bad day when he found himself in a pit with a lion on a snowy day.

God uses our setbacks to set us up. God uses our everyday experiences to build our resume. He uses the bad days to position us and get us where he wants us to go. That ought to give us a sense of destiny even when our circumstances don't make sense.

No Sense

I love the point blank honesty of Job 7:16. Job's world comes completely undone financially, relationally, physically, and spiritually. And Job just says it like it is: "**My life makes no sense.**"

Every single person reading this will, at some point in their life, feel what Job felt. No exceptions. Your life will not make sense. You'll be blindsided by a doctor's diagnosis or the police will come knocking on your door or your boss will leave a pink slip on your desk one day. And when it happens it will shake your confidence in God and your confidence in yourself. And you will feel what Job felt.

Job 7:1 says, "How mankind must struggle. A man's life is long and hard. How he grinds on to the end of the week and his wages. **And so to me also have been allotted**

months of frustration and these long and weary nights. When I get to bed I think, 'Oh that it was morning,' and then I toss till dawn. My life drags by—day after hopeless day."

Job hit rock bottom and he didn't bounce. And I hope that isn't depressing. I hope it's reassuring. You need to know that you're not alone. You're not abnormal. You're normal.

Immunity

I love the raw honesty of *Bruce Almighty*. In fact, I found the movie more honest about God than some churches. I think too many churches are places where you have to pretend that everything is alright. But that isn't reality.

Some people assume that when they start following Christ they ought to live happily ever after, but I love Phillip Yancey's perspective. **"I used to believe that Christianity solved problems and made life easier. Increasingly, I believe that my faith complicates my life, in ways it should be complicated."**

Here's my point: **spiritual maturity does not equal immunity**. I'm not saying that living inside the guardrails of God's will won't save you lots of headaches and heartaches. It will. But we aren't immune to the harsh realities of life! Life is complicated and confusing. But that is precisely why God sent the Holy Spirit. He helps us navigate the unexpected twists and turns of life.

Sometimes we fall into this fallacy that the more holy we become the less confusion and frustration we'll experience. But it's tough to read the book of Job and still hold that belief. God himself said in Job 1:8 that Job was "blameless" and "upright." And in God's own words, "There is no one else on earth like him." Job is in a class by himself. He was the holiest man on earth at that time in human history!

My question is this: did his holiness equate to less confusion and frustration? The answer is "No." And it's not what I want to hear and it's not what you want to hear, but here is what I'm trying to communicate: maturity does not equal immunity. No matter how mature you become spiritually, you're not immune to "months of frustration" or "long weary nights."

I'm a connoisseur of biographies and one of the common denominators I see is this: **the people that God uses in the greatest ways have dark nights of the soul.**

The *Washington Times* recently did an article on the beatification of Mother Teresa. The title was somewhat portentous: "Research reveals a dark side of Mother Teresa." The article cited some of the dark seasons in Mother Teresa's life where she felt abandoned by God.

The reporter wrote, "Her exterior buoyancy masked an astonishing secret—known only to a small number of clergy counselors but no other close colleagues—that was revealed only through research for her sainthood candidacy." The article went on to cite some of those secrets in her private writings. "I am told that God lives in me—and yet the reality of darkness and coldness and emptiness is so great that nothing touches my soul." What I found interesting is that the author of the article seemed to think that we as readers would be shocked. I wasn't surprised at all because she was human. And maturity doesn't equal immunity.

Admission Ticket

Let me take it a step further. Maybe spiritual growth doesn't result in things getting easier! Maybe it results in things getting tougher. Let me put it in terms of decision making. I love Henry Kissinger's perspective on success. He said, "**Every success is an admission ticket to a new set of decisions**." And those decisions don't get easier. They get harder. Success equals bigger and tougher decisions.

Think about it in political terms. Mayors make decisions that primarily affect a city population. Governors make decisions that reverberate across an entire state. And if you go all the way up the political ladder, Presidents make decisions that send shockwaves across the country and around the world. And all I'm asking is this: does it get easier or harder? Is it easier being a mayor or governor or president? The stakes only get higher. Success equals bigger and tougher decisions.

What is true politically is true spiritually. As God expands your sphere of influence it doesn't get easier. It gets harder. The larger NCC becomes the harder it gets because I feel the cumulative responsibility and accountability of leading the church. The choices aren't getting easier. They are getting harder.

The more kids you have the tougher it gets. The wealthier you become the tougher it is to manage your financial portfolio. When you get that promotion at work, the job doesn't get any easier because the stakes become higher. But that's a good thing.

The reward in the parable of the talents wasn't an all-expenses-paid vacation or early retirement. The master said, "You have been faithful with a few things, I'll put you in charge of many things."

In the kingdom of God, **the reward for good work is more work!** So my prayer is not that your life would get easier. My prayer for you is this: that you would be faced with bigger and tougher decisions because that is evidence of spiritual growth.

Wild Goose Chase

One of our core values at National Community Church is **expect the unexpected**. God is predictably unpredictable!

Oswald Chambers said, **"To be certain of God means that we are uncertain in all our ways, we do not know what a day may bring forth."**

Celtic Christians had a great name for the Holy Spirit. It sounds sacrilegious at first earshot, but I've learned to love it. They called the Holy Spirit **the Wild Goose**. I can't think of a better description of "being led by the Spirit" than a wild goose chase.

That's what it feels like and according to Jesus that's exactly what it is. In John 3:8, Jesus says, "The wind blows wherever it pleases. You hear its sound, but you cannot tell where it comes from or where it is going. So it is with everyone born of the Spirit."

There is part of us that wants predictability and familiarity and stability, but that's not Jesus offers. He said that foxes have dens, but he didn't know where he was going to sleep at the end of each day! Read the gospels and you come to the conclusion that Jesus was predictably unpredictable.

And nothing has changed. Following Jesus is full of surprises! When you follow Jesus, **anything can happen!**

Fall-Back Positions

I have passages of Scripture that I refer to as fall-back positions. A fall-back position is your safety net when you fall financially or emotionally or spiritually. Proverbs 16:9 is one of my fall-back positions. I lean on this verse all the time when my compass needle is spinning. **"In his heart a man plans his course, but the Lord orders his steps."**

You may think you know where you're headed but you have no idea! John Chancellor said, **"If you want to make God laugh, tell him your plans."**

The good news is that God knows where you're going. And He knows how to get you there emotionally, physically, intellectually, and spiritually.

God is in the business of strategically positioning us in the right place at the right time. The when, where, and why of your life are anything but accidental. They are providential. And that perspective makes all the difference in the world.

Acts 17:26 says, "From one man He made every nation of men, that they should inhabit the whole earth: and he determined the times set for them and the exact places where they should live." In other words, we live where we live and we live when we live by divine design. **Our chronology and geography are ordained by God.**

Open Doors

I've found from personal experience that the right place at the right time often feels like the wrong place at the wrong time. I'll never forget an incident that happened in September of 1996. NCC was a neophyte church meeting in a DC public school. I was out of town checking voicemail and discovered that our school was being closed down because of fire code violations—effective immediately. I wish I could say that I responded in faith, but here's what I wrote in my journal. "We've been backed into a corner."

We hardly felt like a church at that point. We were a ragtag group of about fifty people on a good Sunday. And we were about to become a homeless church. What I didn't know is that God was about to open an unbelievable door of opportunity.

I had no idea at the time, but the week I met with management, AMC theaters had initiated a nationwide program promoting the use of its theaters during non-movie hours. As far as I know, we were the first organization to respond to that promotion and we didn't even know it existed. It was like God rolled out the red carpet and held the door open. All we had to do was walk through it.

One of my favorite passages and one of my favorite prayers is Revelation 3:7. "These are the words of him who is holy and true, who holds the key of David. **What he opens no one can shut, and what he shuts no one can open.** I know your deeds. See, I have placed before you an open door that no one can shut."

That passage is an allusion back to Isaiah 22:22. As mayor of David's palace, Eliakim wore the key to the house of David around his shoulder. The key was a symbol of authority. He was the only person in the palace who had access to every room. There was no door that he could not lock or unlock. Eliakim is a type of Christ who now holds the key of David. There is no door that Jesus cannot open or close.

God closes doors for numerous reasons, but here are two of them. Sometimes He closes doors **to get us to consider other options**. And sometimes He closes doors **to get us to transition** from one place or one thing to another place or another thing.

If God hadn't closed the door at the DC public school we would have never considered the movie theaters @

Union Station. In retrospect, it's tough to imagine a more strategic spiritual beachhead.

Occasionally, someone will ask me when NCC is going to get its own building. The unspoken sentiment is that you aren't a "real church" until you have a church building. I went into church planting with the traditional mindset. I assumed that we'd buy or build a building at some point. I'm not so sure anymore. Now my first thought when people ask when we're getting a church building is, "Have you seen our building?"

We've got nine theaters, forty food court, and dozens of retail shops right outside our front door. When it was built in 1903, Union Station was the largest room under one roof so I think it's safe to say that we've got the largest foyer of any church in the country. We have our own metro system and parking garage. We've even got our own railroad for that matter!

Close to 100,000 people pass through Union Station on a daily basis! God has strategically positioned NCC in the middle of the marketplace. Why would we want a "church" when we've got this?

George MacLeod said, "**The cross must be raised again at the center of the marketplace as well as on the steeple of the church.** I am claiming that Jesus was not crucified in a cathedral between two candles, but on a cross between two thieves; on the town garbage heap, at a crossroads so cosmopolitan they had to write His title in Hebrew, Latin, and Greek. At the kind of place where cynics talk smut, and thieves curse, and soldiers gamble, because that is where He died and that is what he died about and that is where churchmen ought to be and what churchmen should be about."

There is a cross over Union Station.

I'll never forget the feeling as I walked out of Union Station the day I signed the lease with the movie theater. I can only describe it as an overwhelming sense of destiny.

Before I left the Station that day I picked up a history of Union Station and the first page told the story of Theodore Roosevelt signing the Bill of Congress to create Union Station on February 28, 1903. It said, "An act of congress to create a Union Station, **and for other purposes**."

That phrase—"and for other purposes"—jumped off the page and into my spirit. A hundred years later, Union Station is serving God's purposes through the ministry of National Community Church. President Roosevelt, the Congress, the architect, and the construction crew thought they were building a train station. God knew they were building a church.

Never Say Die

I believe that our prayers are eternal—they never die!

My grandfather used to pray for us at night. The reason I know is that I heard him. He was hard of hearing so he couldn't hear himself pray, but everybody else could. Those prayers are still being answered in my life thirty years later. There have been times in my life when the Holy Spirit has spoken to my spirit and said, "The prayers of your grand-father are being answered in your life right now." Our prayers are one of the few things that outlive us.

I believe that every good thing that happens in our lives is an answer to someone's prayer—often prayed long before we were born! And our prayers will bear fruit at some point in the future.

A few months ago I was speaking to pastors and church planters and I met a gentleman who told me that he went to Washington, DC with a group of Christian square dancers for Jimmy Carter's inauguration in 1976. They came to the visitor center which used to be located in Union Station before its renovation in the 1980's. It literally sat right above the movie theaters where NCC meets on Sundays. He proceeded to tell me that they prayed that a church would be planted in that place! I think he was overwhelmed to discover that their prayers had been answered. And knowing that we were an answer to those prayers deepened my sense of destiny! Those prayers were answered more than twenty years after they were initially prayed. Our prayers have no expiration date!

On the sixtieth anniversary of D-Day, June 6, 2004, the following article appeared in the Sunday edition of the *Washington Post*. It was researched and written by Georgetown professor Jim Moore.

> *Shortly after midnight on June 6, 1944, America awoke to the news that Allied troops had just landed on the beaches of Normandy. Charles Wilson, the CEO of General Electric, arrived at Washington's Union Station early that morning to meet a colleague. As he walked onto the bustling concourse, through which more than 100,000 people passed every day, he felt a sense of expectancy in the air. Soon the news quietly being passed from person to person reached him: The invasion was underway. Wilson, describing that day years later in a magazine article, remembered the powerful effect of the news on him and commuters throughout the station.*
>
> *Looking off into the distance, he noticed a woman sitting on a hard wooden bench quietly fall to her knees to pray. A businessman seated next to her quickly followed, and Wilson watched as soon one person after another knelt and began to pray in silence. The scene was repeated spontaneously throughout the terminal, turning Union Station for a few fleeting moments into what*

*Wilson described as a "house of worship."
Then the audible hush that had fallen over
the station lifted as people returned to their
business, going off in separate directions.*

I emailed Jim Moore because I thought he'd like to know that sixty years later Union Station serves as a "house of worship" every Sunday! He wrote back and said, "Thank you so much for your email. I was delighted to hear of your ministry at Union Station and Ballston. I was very touched by that story from D-Day, and clearly you are the inheritor of that tradition."

Our prayers outlive us. They don't die when we die. They are the inheritance we leave to those whom we pray for. And the chain reaction our prayers cause will be the most startling revelation on the other side of eternity!

Oswald Chambers said, **"As we obey the leadings of the Spirit of God, we enable God to answer the prayers of other people. I mean that our lives, my life, is the answer to someone's prayer, prayed perhaps centuries ago."**

Roll the Dice

Esther is a study in contrasts. Esther 3:7 says that Haman and Xerxes "cast the pur" to determine when the execution would happen. The literally rolled the dice. That is the ancient version of, "Eeney meeney miney moe; catch a tiger by the toe." But Einstein said, **"God doesn't play dice."** There is no guesswork involved. God's timing is perfect.

A few years ago I was going through our connection cards and one card caught my attention. The box that said first time visitor was checked and under the section that said, "How did you hear about National Community Church?" this person wrote, "I met the pastor at blockbuster video." There's a first for everything!

I couldn't help but think that God works in strange and

mysterious ways. I actually remembered meeting this woman. We were both standing at the checkout counter at Blockbuster and she noticed my watch with our logo. At the end of our conversation I invited her to church. She came and wrote me this email afterwards.

Pastor Mark,

We met at the Blockbuster Video in Hechinger Mall. I made a comment about what an interesting watch you were wearing. I said to my father a couple months ago, I'm all churched out. There's got to be more than singing in the choir or being on a committee. Last Sunday, I was compelled to be at National Community Church. It was everything I needed to hear. Your message on Sunday and my reading this week has changed my entire life and mindset. I've lost count of how many times I have read the bulletin and really tried to see how it applies to my life. There is a spirit of freedom that I hadn't felt in a long time. I felt truly free to openly praise and worship the Lord, which is what I have been lacking for a long, long period of time. I sincerely believe Jesus gave me a "divine appointment". I'm glad I listened to the Holy Spirit and did not let anything keep me from coming to NCC. I'm looking forward to church this Sunday and I haven't been able to say that in a long time!

Sometimes my imagination gets a little carried away, but I envision an angelic staff meeting and one of the agenda items is divine appointments.

One of the angels says, "Delvara is churched out." Another angel recommends the church @ Union Station (wishful thinking, I know). The angel in charge of research puts our names into a search engine on his database and comes back a few minutes later. "Well, I think there is only one way they are going to cross paths. There is only one thing they have in common. They are both members of the blockbuster video at Hechinger Mall." And they set up a divine appointment!

I don't know if that's exactly how it happens, but I do know that there is no way I could have orchestrated a meeting like that with someone I don't even know. But God is in the business of strategically positioning us in the right place at the right time.

One Step

God's will is usually revealed **one step at a time**. Sometimes I wish God would give us the twenty-five year plan, but he doesn't do it because his primary goal isn't a long-range vision, but daily dependence on him. And when we live in daily dependence on Him we always end up where God wants us to go.

Life is full of what I call **one small step, one giant leap moments**.

I'll never forget watching my oldest son, Parker, take his first step. It was November 11, 1996. We were having dinner with friends in Baltimore, Maryland and their home was the perfect environment for beginning walkers: a plush carpet with thick padding. It was much more forgiving than the hardwood floors in our DC row house. Parker stood on his wobbly legs and I practically willed him to walk. I called to him with conviction in my voice and held out my arms. Then it happened. With a Herculean effort, my year-old son put one foot in front of the other and entered the world of the walking!

It was the greatest moment of his short-lived life: his first step. What is now so simple was so complicated. What is now so easy was so difficult. What is now so commonplace was so special. We lost all inhibition and celebrated my son's very small, very big accomplishment.

The first step is the most important. And the first step is the toughest.

Uhaul

After Seminary, my wife and I were trying to figure out our next step. We didn't know what to do, but an opportunity opened up in Washington, DC. We were living in the Chicago area at time. That's where we both grew up and we had no intentions of leaving, but a failed church plant opened us up to anything. We prayed about it. We sensed God calling us to DC. In fact, the day we made the decision to move to DC I went to my mailbox on campus and there was a postcard from George Washington University. Why they sent me a postcard I have no idea? Our going had nothing to do with GW. But the front of the card said, "Your future is in Washington, DC." I can be pretty dense sometimes, but even I couldn't miss that confirmation!

When I think about all the good things that have happened in our lives since we moved to DC I can't help but think that none of it would have happened if we had stayed in Chicago. We had no guaranteed salary when we moved. We didn't have a place to live. We just loaded up our Uhaul and moved to DC because we sensed God guiding us there. And every good thing that has happened since then can be traced back to that one small step, one giant leap.

Hebrews 11:8 says, 'By faith, Abraham, when called to go to a place he would later receive as his inheritance, obeyed and went, even though he did not know where he was going."

Abraham has no idea where he's going! It was a wild

goose chase. But he stepped out in faith anyways. Israel traces its history back to that one small step, one giant leap of faith.

The Fear of Failure

A few years ago our family joined a community pool and the first time I took my kids swimming my daughter, Summer, started jumping off the side into the pool. I could tell my son, Parker, wanted to jump but he was afraid. He was standing on the edge of the pool and I finally said, "Parker, why don't you jump?" In classic kidspeak, Parker said, "My legs won't move." His brain was yelling "jump" but his legs said "no way." I said, "Why don't you let me hold your hand on the first jump." And the rest is history! By the end of the summer, Parker was doing cannon balls and 180's and head-first dives. That first jump is always the toughest.

The first time you share your faith or start a business or ask someone on a date it's scary because you've never done it before. But we need to face those fears. John Ortberg says, **"God has an inextinguishable habit of asking people to do things that are scary to them."**

Here's what I think: the cure for the fear of failure isn't success. **The cure for the fear of failure is failure**. The cure for the fear of rejection isn't acceptance. The cure for the fear of rejection is rejection.

Allergies are a perfect analogy. The way you treat allergies is by exposing yourself to small quantities of the allergen so that you build up immunity. If you're allergic to failure you need to fail a few times.

I've always had a fear of failure. Like most people, I want guaranteed success. One of the greatest things to happen to me was to fall flat on my face trying to plant a church on Chicago's north shore during seminary. It was embarrassing. It was disillusioning. But it was good for me. I'm grateful it happened because we ended up in DC as a result and I know that's where God wanted us. That experience helped cure my fear of failure. I still don't like failing, but I'm not afraid of it anymore. One of our buzzwords at NCC is "experiment." We are trying new things all the time. We're just not afraid to fail because we approach everything as an experiment that we can learn from. To be perfectly honest, failure can be funny. I love looking back and laughing at those failures that weren't funny at the time!

One of the low points in NCC history was one of the first concerts we hosted at our coffeehouse on Capitol Hill. We invited a seven-member band and I expected about seventy-five people. I was sitting with the band in our green room and two minutes before the concert started I went to check on things. There were four people there! I was dying! I've never wanted the rapture to happen so badly in my life! Not only was it a failure, but the honorarium was $750. That works out to $175 bucks a head. It was a quantum failure, but it was also funny!   Not at the time. But it is now. More people in the band than the audience! That's funny stuff.

Near-Death

I celebrate my birthday on November 5 each year, but I have another birthday. Around midnight on July 23, 2000, I woke up with abdominal pain. I went to aftercare but the doctors couldn't diagnose the problem so I went home. After a sleepless night I tried to preach a message that Sunday morning, but I walked out doubled over in pain. After x-rays and an MRI they finally discovered that my intestines had ruptured. What was in my intestines filled my abdominal cavity and was poisoning me to death. I could tell by the look on the surgeon's face that this could be it. Honestly, I was in so much pain that part of me wanted to die. But God spared my life. I was rushed into emergency surgery and survived on a respirator for two days. After several surgeries, eight days in the hospital, and weeks of recovery I was almost as good as new.

During my recovery process I read Oswald Chamber's biography, *Abandoned to* God. Part of the reason it impacted me so profoundly is that Chambers died from an internal rupture not unlike mine. It made me feel even more fortunate that I had survived.

In his biography, Chambers talked about parentheses. He said, "A parenthesis is a sentence inserted into an otherwise grammatically complete sentence, and if you want to understand the author, pay particular attention to the parenthesis. God puts a parenthesis in the middle flow of our life, life goes on before and after, but if you want to understand the life, read the parenthesis, if you can."

I wrote in my journal, "I feel like this is a parenthesis in my life—life goes on before and after—but there is something God wants to do in me during this parenthesis in my life that can't be done any other way."

Walter Kaufman said, "**It makes for a better life if one has a rendezvous with death**." July 23, 2000 was my rendezvous with death. It was the worst day of my life. It was also the best day. I'm not who I was! "Tragedy, even in everyday life, can be a valuable form of restructuring," notes Thomas Moore. "It is painful and in some ways destructive, but is also puts things in a new order."

Maybe you're in the middle of a parenthesis in your life. You're between jobs or between relationships or between places. You get papers or a diagnosis or an email that tells you what you don't want to know. Those are challenging circumstances.

God doesn't expect you to roll out the red carpet, inviting tragedy into your life. But God uses those experiences if we allow Him to.

I read a magazine poll recently and eighty-seven percent of the people interviewed said that a painful event—death of a loved one, illness, breakup, divorce—helped them find more positive meaning in life. In the words of Calvin Miller, we discover that "**the worst and best days of my life could be one**."

Oliver Wendell Holmes, who served as a Supreme Court Justice from 1902-1932, was as full of passion when he retired at ninety-one as when he was appointed to the bench at sixty-one. His life was forever marked by three near-death experiences during the civil war. Seriously wounded three times, he said, "It was given us to learn at the outset that life is a profound and passionate thing."

"I notice a trend that seems almost universal in the reminiscences of older people," says Philip Yancey. "They tend to recall difficult times with a touch of nostalgia." According to one poll of Londoners, sixty percent of those who survived the Blitz Kreig—the relentless bombing by German airplanes—now remember that time as the happiest period of their lives.

Grandparents love to talk about the Great Depression and its accompanying hardships. They share stories about midnight trips to the outhouse in sub-zero temperatures, three mile jaunts through knee-deep snow just to get to school (and it was uphill both ways), and having to eat fast enough to get a second-helping because there were twelve siblings. Or was that fifteen? Difficult experiences that may have humbled us at the time, conjure feelings of pride with the passing of years.

Crisis moments are defining moments. They can make us or break us. It's up to us. The word crisis in the Chinese language has two characters—one means "danger" and the other "opportunity."

Most of us wouldn't want to relive our darkest moments, but we aren't willing to trade them either. They teach us invaluable lessons that cannot be learned any other way. They help make us who we are.

Act III: The Challenge

-→═◦⊂═→-

*It is better to hated for who you are than
loved for who you are not.*

Andre Gide

The more you base your identity on who God is and
what God can do the less you have to prove yourself.
Part of discovering who you are is coming to terms with
who you're not. When John the Baptist was asked if he was
the Messiah, he didn't claim to be who he wasn't. He
accepted his lot in life. "A man can only have what is given
him from Heaven." When his followers left him to go follow
Jesus he said, "He must become greater and I must become
less." John knew who he was. And he knew who he wasn't.

True freedom is having nothing to prove. You don't have
to be the best at everything. You don't have to be right every
time. You don't have to have everything figured out all the
time. You have the freedom to fail. You have the freedom to
be wrong. You have the freedom to doubt.

The more and more I become like Christ the more and

more aware I become of my sinfulness—especially my motives. But as I become more aware of my sinfulness I become more aware of God's grace! Here is the fundamental mistake many of us make: we minimize sinfulness and thereby minimize mercy. But it's only when we realize the full extent of our sin that we appreciate the full extent of God's mercy!

C.S. Lewis said it this way. "When a man is getting better he understands more and more clearly the evil that is still left in him. When a man is getting worse he understands his own badness less and less."

If you're getting better you understand that.

If you aren't you don't.

Approval Addicts

A few years ago, my oldest son, Parker, graduated from Kindergarten and it was quite the ordeal complete with diploma and ceremony. During one part of the ceremony each child shared their dream. Parker was the last one to share his dream so we anxiously waited to hear what he would say. My six year-old said, "I want the whole world to know Jesus." Lora and I started crying tears of joy! We could have died and gone to heaven! It was the pinnacle of parenthood. All our hard work had paid off! Unfortunately, the story doesn't end there.

I asked Parker about his dream afterwards and he popped our balloon when he told us that the teachers told them what to say! But it gets worse. He said, "That isn't really my dream." I asked him what his dream was. He said, "I want to be a construction man."

If I had to choose between the two dreams I'd probably pick the whole world knowing Jesus, but what I love about that is this: Parker wasn't trying to be who I wanted him to be. I don't want him to be what I want him to be. I want him to be what God wants him to be and that may be what I want him to be but it may not.

I think too many people try to be who everyone wants them to be, but that is a formula for frustration.

The Pulitzer Prize winning journalist, Henry Bayard Swope said, "**I cannot give you a formula for success, but I can give you a formula for failure: Try to please everybody.**"

Here's what I know about kids: kids don't try to be who they're not. They haven't learned the adult art of disguising themselves yet.

Michael Lewis said it this way. "**Children enjoy one big advantage over adults; they haven't decided who they are. They haven't sunk a lot of psychological capital into a particular self.**"

To become like little children is to stop pretending to be someone you're not.

Samuel Johnson so aptly said, "**Almost every man wastes part of his life in attempts to display qualities which he does not possess.**"

Part of discovering who you are is coming to terms with who you're not. Our inabilities and disabilities can define us or we can define them. They can become the source of an inferiority complex or we can laugh at them.

I am affectionately known as *Mr. Unhandy Man* to my close friends and family. If you ask me to put up a shelf you might as well ask me to build the whole house. I'm inept.

Maybe I can't assemble an entertainment center in five tries. Maybe I can't find a stud with a stud finder. Maybe I can't paint perfectly straight lines. Maybe I can't assemble a grill in less than four hours. So what? All of us are bad at something! Those inabilities are opportunities to laugh at ourselves!

I'm convinced **the healthiest and holiest people are those who laugh at themselves the most.** Some of us just have more potential than others!

The words humor and humility have the same etymological roots. **Humor is a form of humility**. It's the opposite of having to prove yourself.

Spiritual maturity is a process of caring less and less about what people think and more and more about what God thinks. I'm not saying that the opinions of people aren't important in certain circumstances, but you can't base your identity on how people feel about you or what people think about you. You've got to base your identity on how God feels and what God thinks about you. Zechariah 2:8 says you are the apple of His eye!

I think of Abraham Lincoln's timeless wisdom when people aren't pleased with me. He said, **"You can please all of the people some of the time, some of the people all of the time, but you can't please all of the people all of the time."**

Approval Addicts

Most of us, when we do something good, look out of the corner of our eye to make sure someone is watching us. That's human nature. A lot of us are what John Ortberg calls **"approval addicts."** We're addicted to the approval of others. It may not be as frowned upon as other addictions, but it can be just as debilitating. **Some people live in bondage to what others think of them**. They are at the mercy of other people's opinions! Ortberg says, "Vast amounts of human behavior, though painstakingly disguised, are simply attempts at showing off. We want to impress other people without letting on that we're trying to impress them."

All of us want to impress others, but nothing is more unimpressive than someone trying to impress others. You know who is really impressive? Someone who isn't trying to impress anybody!

Our attempts to impress others reveal insecurity. The more insecure we are the more we try to impress people.

Approval addiction is tough to break, but the key is caring more and more about what God thinks.

Identity Traps

There are three identity traps that most of us fall into. Almost like a camouflaged covering over a pit, we blindly stumble into these traps and end up in a pit of despair. We try to climb out of the pit by doing what got us in there in the first place. And the hole seems to get deeper and deeper the harder and harder we try!

The first pit is the **performance trap**. The performance trap is basing your identity on **what you can do**. The problem with that is this: you're only as good as your last performance. If your poll numbers or sales numbers or financial numbers go down you go down with them.

The second pit is the **comparison trap**. The comparison trap is basing your identity on **how you stack up with others**. The problem with that is this: our comparisons always result in one of two extremes—pride or jealously. And neither one is healthy or holy.

The third pit is the **impression trap**. The impression trap is basing your identity on **other people's opinions of you**. The problem with that is this: you can't impress everybody all the time. And part of the problem with other people's opinion of you is that they aren't omniscient.

There are **four kinds of people** in your life—people who **like you for the right reasons**; people who **like you for the wrong reasons**; people who **don't like for the wrong reasons**; and people who **don't like you for the right reasons**.

Most of us put too much stock in the people who don't like us for the wrong reasons.

Validation

A few months ago I was headed to a Bible study with a

government official who you would know by name. Security is pretty tight getting into government buildings these days and the higher up someone is the tougher it is to get in the door. I've been going to these Bible studies for years so I didn't anticipate any problems. I pulled up to the security gate and told the security guard who I was and who I was meeting with. And the guard sort of smirked. It was an interesting response. I don't know if it was the way I looked or the car I was driving or what I said, but it was almost like he didn't believe I was who I said I was or that I was meeting with who I said I was meeting with.

He asked for ID, checked the computer, and evidently I wasn't in there so he called in another guard and I could see them talking and I literally saw them shake their heads and laugh. At this point I'm feeling a little defensive.

They told me to back up and park on the street which I'd never had to do before and it was a little embarrassing. I'm sitting there feeling like a fool and another guard approaches my car like I'm a suspected terrorist. He asked me to make a phone call which I did. And it turns out that this government official who I was meeting with had a change in agenda which happens quite often, but I'm typically notified.

I know these guards were just doing their job, but the entire time there was part of me that wanted to be validated and vindicated. I wanted to wave at these guards as they opened the gate and let me in!

Instead of getting in I had to ask for my license back and then drive away with my tailpipe between my tires. And the worst thing about it is that these guards didn't know why I was leaving! They probably had another laugh at my expense.

That incident got under my skin so I did an **emotional autopsy**. Here's what I found. I wanted to prove that I was who I said as I was, but I am who I am whether these security guards believed me or not, laughed at me or not, let me in or not. So I had a choice to make: I could let it get under my skin or I could just laugh about it.

You have a choice to make in circumstances like that. You don't get invited to the party. Your friend gets the promotion instead of you. Someone else gets credit for what you did or you get blamed for what someone else did.

How do you handle those situations? It depends on what you base your identity on. If you base your identity on the opinions of people, it'll get under your skin or you'll try to put them in their place or you'll try to even the score. You'll try to prove yourself over and over again. And you'll never measure up.

But if you base your identity on who God is you can laugh at yourself.

Proof

Here's a thought. Jesus never tried to prove who He was. He proclaimed that he was the Son of God, but when people asked for proof he didn't give it to them. Here's why. He knew when a question was asked for the wrong reasons. He saw right through false motives. But it goes deeper than that. Jesus also knew that you can't prove yourself to other people. All you can do is be who you are. And people can accept you or reject you on those terms.

Jesus put the ball in the disciple's court in Matthew 16:15. It is the relational litmus test. "Who do you say that I am?"

Many Christians mistakenly think that spiritual maturity is proving themselves to God. **Spiritual maturity is God proving Himself to us over and over and over again until we finally have faith in His faithfulness.** It comes back to what you base your identity on. It's not about what you can do for God. It's about what God can do for you.

The more you base your identity on who God is and what God can do the less you have to prove yourself to people. And the corollary is obvious. **The more you base your identity on who you are and what you can do the**

more you have to prove yourself to people. And you have to do it day in and day out.

It's so tiring having to be the best, having to be right, having to be perfect all the time. There is so much freedom in not having to be the best at everything, being wrong and admitting it, admitting and laughing at your imperfections. It takes all the pressure off!

Not too long ago I was at the gas station and a guy asked for directions to Gaithersburg, Maryland. I gave him directions, but another guy overheard us and said, "There's a better way." I have to admit that I got a little defensive at first. There is no better way! I'm Mapquest Man! I'm the Human Onstar! It's my way or the highway, buddy!

And then it dawned on me that I didn't have to be right. Worst case scenario was that I didn't know the best route and I'd learn a better one. I don't have to be the world's greatest direction-giver. I can actually stop and ask for directions if I need them!

Those ceaseless attempts to prove ourselves in the little things drains the energy out of us like a car battery with the lights left on. You can try to prove yourself to everybody, but it is so tiring having to be right all the time. There is so much freedom in not being the best at everything, not being right about everything. **There is so much freedom in embracing our imperfections instead of trying to prove we are who we aren't.**

The more you base your identity on God the less you have to prove. The more you base your identity on you the more you have to prove. **True freedom is having nothing to prove because your find your identity in Christ.** He becomes our soul sufficiency.

Monument to Himself

Saul and David were both Kings of Israel, but they are a study in contrasts.

Let me put Saul on the couch first.

Two verses represent two defining moments in Saul's life. The first one is I Samuel 14:35. "Saul **built an altar to the Lord,** the first one he had ever built." So far so good! At this point in his term of office he is giving credit where credit is due. He is serving the one who anointed Him King in the first place. But something happens between I Samuel 14:35 and I Samuel 15:12. It is the beginning of the end. "Early the next morning Samuel went to find Saul. Someone told him, 'Saul went to Carmel to **set up a monument to himself'**."

Saul stopped building altars to God and started building monuments to himself.

Samuel sees right through Saul. He says in verse 17, "Although you may **think little of yourself,** are you not the leader of the tribes of Israel?"

Let me tell you who builds monuments to themselves: its people who think little of themselves. Let me say it another way. **Pride is a byproduct of insecurity. The more insecure you are the more monuments you have to build.** If you're really insecure, all you do is build monuments to yourself all the time. Eventually you don't have time to do anything else!

People who are insecure build monuments to themselves. People who feel a sense of security build altars to God.

I Samuel 9:1 says that Saul came from a rich and influential family. It says, "Saul was the most handsome man in Israel—head and shoulders taller than anyone else." He had Hollywood looks and an NBA physique. He was a skilled warrior and anointed prophet. And Saul is chosen by God as the first King of Israel. So he's the best-looking and most-powerful guy in Israel. He has fame. He has fortune. This guy was the complete package. Saul is da man!

I don't know of anybody who had fewer reasons to be

jealous! And yet, when I survey Scripture, I don't find anybody who was more insanely jealous. Saul was insecurity personified. And that deep-seated insecurity was his Achilles Heel.

David enters the story stage right in I Samuel 17. After defeating Goliath, David ends up on center stage. And it says that David was successful in everything he did so Saul kept promoting him in the ranks. David was the best thing that happened to Saul's administration, but Saul begins to perceive David as a threat.

The Israelites are coming home from battle and the people line the streets like a ticker-tape parade. And they sing a song. And we actually have those ancient lyrics recorded in I Samuel 18:7. They sang, "Saul has killed his thousands, and David his tens of thousands!" Saul hated that song. Every time it came on the radio he'd change the station. He couldn't handle David's success. And his insecurity got the best of him. His mind started playing tricks on him and he started imagining worst case scenarios. We have one of them recorded in I Samuel 18:8. "They credit David with tens of thousands and me with only thousands. Next they'll be making him their king!" And it says, **So from that time on Saul kept a jealous eye on David.**"

Saul forgot who anointed him king! He wasn't elected by the people. He was anointed by God. Instead of basing his identity on his anointing—the fact that he was chosen by God to lead the people of Israel. Saul was basing his identity on his performance in battle. And along comes David. And he outperforms Saul. Saul loses his mind, loses his soul, and loses his kingdom because of his insane jealousy. But all of his problems are the byproduct of basing his identity on the wrong thing.

The Comparison Game

I'm a competitive person. I don't like losing *Candyland*

to my kids! But that competitive streak is dangerous to my spiritual health. It can totally distort my motives so that I do the right thing for the wrong reasons. Ecclesiastes 4:4 says, "Then I observed that most people are motivated to success by their envy of their neighbors. But this too is meaningless, like chasing the wind."

Lots of people are successful for lots of different reasons, but here's the catch. **If you achieve success for the wrong reasons you won't enjoy it.** Enough will never be enough. I like the way Richard Foster said it. "The lust for affluence is psychotic. It is psychotic because it has completely lost touch with reality. We crave things we do not need or enjoy. We buy things we do not want to impress people we do not like."

Saul was playing the comparison game, but here's the problem with the comparison game. No one wins. There are only two potential outcomes. Comparison always results in one of two extremes—pride or jealousy. And neither one is healthy or holy.

Either you will compare yourself with people who are somehow "worse than you" and it'll result in pride or you'll compare yourself with someone who is "better than you" and you'll sink in the quicksand of jealousy.

There is a third option.

You can quit trying to prove yourself. You can quit competing. You can quit comparing. And you can base your identity on what Christ has done for you. And when you do, you'll experience a joy and freedom and peace that the world can't give and the world can't take away!

The Armrest Test

I think there are two ways to approach life. **You can act as if everything belongs to you** or **you can act as if nothing belongs to you.** You know where I think this reveals itself? On airplanes!

The only thing between you and a total stranger is the armrest. Without exception there is the obligatory jockeying for armrest position. The problem is that there aren't any rules for this kind of thing. There are no books on armrest protocol.

Who does it belong to? Does it belong to whoever gets there first? Does it belong whoever is larger? If you get up and go to the lavatory do you forfeit all rights to the armrest? Is it ok if your arms touch? These are tough issues! It's not like they give you one bag of peanuts or one drink or one magazine and you have to figure out who gets it. But there it is in between the two of you—one armrest.

I think you can tell a lot about a person by how they treat the armrest. You know what drives me crazy? Someone who acts as if the armrest belongs to them! They never stop jockeying for position.

The armrest test is a microcosm. Here's the point: **you can live your life as if everything belongs to you, but you'll spend the rest of your life jockeying for position**. You'll never be able to rest or relax. You'll always be comparing and competing. And to be perfectly honest, that makes for a miserable trip!

James 4:1 says, "What is causing the quarrels and fights among you? Isn't it the whole army of evil desires at war within you? **You want what you don't have**, so you scheme and kill to get it. You are jealous of what others have, and you can't possess it, so you fight and quarrel to take it away from them."

Translation: **almost all of our problems are the result of wanting what isn't ours and jockeying for position to get it**! The Biblical word is covetousness and it takes lots of different forms. You can want their money or their position or their face or their spouse, but the common denominator is wanting what isn't yours.

Most of our problems would resolve themselves if we

simply acted as if nothing belonged to us!
The epicenter of stewardship is this fundamental conviction that nothing belongs to you.
Even you don't belong to you!

Borrowed Breath

The Screwtape Letters is a fictional account of the Devil mentoring a novice demon named Wormwood on some of his age-old tactics. The Devil says, **"The sense of ownership is always to be encouraged. The more claims on life, therefore, that your patient can be induced to make, the more often he will feel injured and, as a result, ill-tempered."**
That's worth reading again.

One of the enemy's ancient tactics is to get us to want what we don't have. It's as old as the Garden of Eden. The entire garden was at their disposal, but Adam and Eve wanted what they couldn't have.

The Devil continues, "Humans are always putting up claims to ownership, which sound equally funny in heaven and in Hell. And all the time the joke is that the word 'Mine' in its fully possessive sense cannot be uttered by a human being about anything. In the long run either Our Father or the Enemy will say 'Mine' of each thing that exists, and specially of each man."

The bottom line is that nothing belongs to you. You didn't bring anything into this world and you won't take anything out. You don't own anything. You live on borrowed time. You live on borrowed breath. And if nothing belongs to you then you have nothing to prove. Everything is a gift from God.

Ownership

The Dutch theologian, Abraham Kuyper, said, **"In the total expanse of human life there is not a single square** inch of which the Christ, who alone is sovereign, does not declare, 'That is mine'!"

I Corinthians 6:20 says, "**You are not your own**; you were bought at a price. Therefore honor God with you body."

Stewardship begins the moment you recognize that you don't belong to you.

I was jogging on the Mall not long ago and passed some women who were part of a march. They wore t-shirts that said, "My body is not public property." The abortion issue comes back, in large part, to the way you view you. If you belong to you, you can do anything you want. But you don't. Your body isn't public property—you don't belong to others. You're body isn't private property—you don't belong to you. **Your body is God's property**.

II Corinthians 1:22 says, "God set his seal of ownership on us, and put his Spirit in our hearts as a deposit, guaranteeing what is to come."

My wife and I purchased our first home in April of 1996. On the day of settlement we signed dozens of documents, the most important of which was the deed. The moment we signed the deed there was a transfer of ownership from seller to buyer. They handed over the keys and we became the legal owners of our home.

In the same sense, there is a transfer of ownership when we decide to follow Christ. We give God the keys. We relinquish control and God assumes responsibility.

Alter Ego

❖══◎══❖

The periodic table is comprised of more than one hundred chemical elements with unique properties. When those elements combine they form a compound. Oxygen and hydrogen are a good example. When you combine one-part oxygen with two-parts hydrogen you end up with H^2O or water.

What's fascinating is that some elements which are poisonous or dangerous as individual elements become extremely helpful or useful when combined with the right counterpart. Chlorine, for example, is a poisonous gas that gives bleach its offensive odor. You don't want to inhale or swallow too much chlorine or it can kill you. Sodium, on the other hand, is extremely dangerous because it is highly flammable. But when you combine chlorine with sodium you get sodium chloride, aka table salt.

John 1:14 says that Jesus was "full of grace and truth." Think of grace as truth as spiritual elements. Grace means **"I'll love you no matter what."** Truth means **"I'll be honest no matter what."**

Truth without grace is poisonous.

Grace without truth is dangerous.

But when you combine them together, they become a powerful spiritual compound. Jesus was the perfect combination of both.

The Real Deal

The word "truth" comes from the Greek word *aletheia* which is two-dimensional. It means "**real**" and "**ideal**." Jesus was both/and. No one was holier. No one was more down-to-earth. He was holy, but he wasn't "holier-than-thou." He didn't put on airs. There was no hidden agenda. There was no pretense. He was the same in private as he was in public.

We live in a culture that craves reality. Millions of Americans tune into dozens of "Reality TV" shows each week. Why? We crave reality. Jesus lived in a very different culture, but the people craved the same thing.

In Luke 19, a distinguished tax collector climbed a tree just to catch a glimpse of Jesus. In Luke 8, a terminally ill woman fought her way through the crowds just to touch the hem of Jesus' garment. In Matthew 15, a crowd of thousands went without food for three days just to listen to Jesus talk. In Mark 2, four men went out of their way to lower a paralytic friend through a hole in the roof just to get to Jesus. And in Luke 7, a prostitute crashed a party, at a Pharisee's house no less, to wash Jesus' feet.

You couldn't keep people away from Jesus! Why? Because they craved reality!

Bruce Barton said, "The essential element in personal magnetism is a consuming sincerity." People were not threatened by Jesus' righteousness. They were attracted to it. His authenticity was irresistible.

Joseph Girzone said Jesus accepted people's "humanness." That's what allowed people "to feel relaxed in his presence." Jesus didn't condone sin, but he didn't expect perfection either. His twelve disciples, handpicked by Jesus himself, had plenty of imperfections.

Sometimes we have a double standard. We publicly preach imperfection—"all have sinned and fallen short." But we privately expect perfection! It's tough to know where to draw the line, but we need to accept "humanness" without condoning sin.

The word "sincere" comes from the Latin phrase *sina cera* which means "without wax." Ancient sculptors used to cover up their imperfections with wax. The wax would disguise their mistakes. A piece of art without defect was *sina cera* or without wax.

Jesus was *sina cera*. His sincerity was magnetic!

The Wizard of Oz

You know what drove Jesus crazy? People who acted like they had it all together! He didn't have the time of day for people who put on an act like everything was alright.

All of us have imperfections, but we have a choice. We can conceal them or reveal them. **True freedom is found when we reveal our imperfections to the right people at the right time**.

Jesus told a story in Luke 18 about two men who went to the Temple to pray. One was a Pharisee and the other a tax collector. "The Pharisee stood up and prayed about himself: 'God, I thank you that I am not like other men—robbers, evildoers, adulterers—even like this tax collector. I fast twice a week and give a tenth of all I get'." But it says, "The tax collector wouldn't even look up." He beat his breast and said, "God, have mercy on me, a sinner."

Jesus said, "I tell you that this man, rather than the other, went home justified before God. For everyone who exalts himself will be humbled and he who humbles himself will be exalted."

I think lots of Christians practice "Wizard of Oz" Christianity. If you've seen the movie you know that the wizard isn't really a wizard. He's a small, old man who is turning dials and flipping switches behind a curtain. Many of us live behind the curtain—**we try to come across as more impressive than we really are.** We're just like the Pharisee in Jesus' story.

We speak in confident tones, but we're full of doubt. We try to appear holy, but lust and anger and greed and pride are at a full boil. We try to look like we've got it all together, but we're filled with guilt and anxiety.

The Veil

II Corinthians 3:13 says, "We are not like Moses, who put a veil over his face so the people of Israel would not see the glory fading away." When Moses came back from his face-to-face meetings with God at the tent of meeting his face was radioactive so he wore a veil. This passage is a debatable, but one take is that Moses kept wearing the veil even when he didn't need to because, like a lot of us, he wanted to appear more spiritual than he really was.

It's called the imposter phenomenon. All of us, at some level, are faking it. But as John Ortberg says, **"The more skillful we are at impression management, the more we are trapped in our true aloneness."**

We've got to pull back the curtain like the tax collector in Luke 18. We need to acknowledge our weaknesses.

I'm convinced that we are more sinful that we realize. Jeremiah 17:9 says, "The heart is deceitful above all things and desperately wicked." I'm also convinced that God is more merciful than we realize.

When we underestimate our sinfulness we underestimate God's mercifulness.

It is our weaknesses that God uses to reveal his power. It is our pain that God turns into spiritual gain. And it is our brokenness and loneliness that God uses to help us minister to others.

God wants us to be real. He's not looking for perfection. He's looking for honesty and transparency and sincerity. The bottom line is this: Jesus reserved his harshest words for those who hid behind the curtain. "For one sin he had no mercy," said Bruce Barton. "He denounced the insincerity of the Pharisees."

Psalm 51:6 says, "You desire truth in the inner parts." God doesn't expect perfection. He does expect gut-wrenching honesty!

Don Everts said, "**Repentance is the alternative to pretending.**"

You can pretend to be perfect or you can repent. It's one or the other!

Too many Christians try to do both and end up in no man's land. Peter Marshall hit the nail on the head. "**We are too Christian really to enjoy sinning and too fond of sinning really to enjoy Christianity.**"

Messy Spirituality

I love the first sentence of Michael Yaconelli's book *Messy Spirituality*. Not too many Christian authors start their books with this sentence: "**My life is a mess.**"

That's a pretty good synopsis of the Psalms. And that is precisely why people love them. There is a raw honesty to them!

Yaconelli said, "For as long as I can remember, I have wanted to be a godly person. Yet when I look at the yesterdays of my life, what I see, mostly, is a broken, irregular path littered with mistakes and failures."

If you were to graph spiritual growth, it wouldn't be a straight line ascending along a forty-five degree angle. There is nothing linear about spiritual growth. Spiritual growth is a jagged line full of ups and downs and awkward angles! It's not nice and neat. It's messy!

Yaconelli says, "**Accepting the reality of our broken,**

flawed lives is the beginning of spirituality." Sometimes we repress our doubts and disappointments, but it only makes them worse. If your conversations with God aren't occasionally laced with anger or frustration or confusion you're probably being disingenuous. God isn't threatened by any of the above. Phillip Yancey is right. "**God prefers honest disagreement to dishonest submission.**"

Washington

Just before she died, Meg Greenfield wrote an insightful book about the psyche of Washington, DC. It's a must-read for Washingtonians. Greenfield spent thirty years as a journalist with the *Washington Post* and she shares her observations in *Washington*. She compares Washington to High School. She said, "**High School is a preeminently nervous place.**" She said that Washington is even worse!

You're always in danger of political extinction. You can't rest on your laurels because there is always someone who has better laurels. You're always up for election.

Meg Greenfield said, "High school is the time when people first contrive to have an image. **It is an attempt to fabricate a whole second persona for public consumption. Life inside the image requires continuous care, feeding and, above all, protection.** That is the worst of it. **It's like never being able to get undressed.** We are, most of us, much of the time, in disguise. **We present ourselves as we think we are meant to be.** In Washington, this is greatly in excess of the ordinary hypocrisies that exist everywhere else."

Transparency doesn't come easy in a place like Washington in the 21st century. There is a lot of pretending. But it didn't come easy in 1st century Jerusalem either. Jesus captured the essence of the Pharisaical heart in Matthew 23:5. "Everything they do is done for men to see." I can summarize the religiosity of the Pharisees in three words—**image was everything**. That's all they cared about. Hold that thought.

Burden of Pretense

In I Kings 14, Jeroboam, the King of Israel, needs to consult the prophet Ahijah, but he wants to do so secretly so he concocts a plan. He says to his wife, "Go disguise, yourself, so you won't be recognized as the wife of Jeroboam. Then go to Shiloh. Ahijah the prophet is there."

As is the case in a lot of Biblical stories, there is a subtle humor. She spends all this time disguising herself and the prophet Ahijah is blind to begin with!

I Kings 14:4 says, "Now Ahijah could not see; his sight was gone because of his age, but the Lord had told Ahijah, 'Jeroboam's wife is coming. When she arrives **she will pretend to be someone else'**."

All of us are guilty of this to one degree or another.

A.W. Tozer said, "**There is hardly a man or woman who dares to be just what he or she is without doctoring up the impression.**" There is nothing wrong with putting our best foot forward, but there is a fine line between making a good first impression and trying to be who we aren't. When we try to be who we're not we experience what Tozer called "**the burden of pretense.**" You can't be yourself.

The wife of Jeroboam arrives. I can picture her double-checking her disguise and rehearsing her lines, but before she even knocks on the door it says, "When Ahijah heard the sound of her footsteps at the door, he said, 'Come in, wife of Jeroboam'."

Busted!

Then the prophet Ahijah asks the $64,000 question in I Kings 14:6, "**Why this pretense?**"

Alter Ego

A few years ago I was walking home from the office and

a friendly neighbor said, "Hi, David." I don't know why, but I just said "hi" back and kept walking. She was so nice and friendly I didn't want to correct her by telling her that my name was actually Mark.

Later that week, the same scenario happened. And again, I didn't have the heart of correct her. To make a long story short, she called me David for two years!

At first, it was sort of fun being David. It was my alter ego. Sometimes I'd walk by with friends and she'd say, "Hi David" and I'd say hi back with a straight face and my friends would get a good laugh. I would explain that she calls me David, and I didn't have the heart to correct her, and it was too late now! So I enjoyed it for a while.

Then one day I thought to myself, "What if she comes to church some Sunday?" And I started getting worried. What if she finds out who I really am? And the fun was replaced with a "burden of pretense." It got awkward. I had to continue to pretend to be who I wasn't. When someone has called you the wrong name a hundred times without correction it's not easy saying, "Oh, by the way, that isn't really my name."

I knew the day of truth would arrive sooner or later. I was walking down the street and I saw this neighbor with a group of neighbors who knew my real name. I could spot trouble a mile away. I wanted to turn around or walk to the other side of the street, but I keep going. The funeral march was playing in my head. As I got closer I knew one of two things was going to happen. Either the other neighbors were going to say, "Hi, Mark." And she was going to look weird at them. Or she was going to say, "Hi, David." And they were going to look weird at her. But either way I was going to look pretty weird. It was a "no win" situation.

Sure enough, she said, "Hi, David." I said, "Hi" back and kept on walking.

I have no idea what was said in the pursuant conversation, but she's never called me David again. In fact, I don't think she says, "Hi" to me anymore!

Here's the thing about pretending: sooner or later you get busted.

There is nothing wrong with putting our best foot forward. The problem is when we try to be what we aren't. It feels pretty good at first. People applaud the image. We like the accolades of appearing to be more than we are. But the end result is that you can never be yourself. You can never let down your guard. You can never really relax or rest.

A.W. Tozer said, **"The rest God offers is the rest of meekness, the blessed relief which comes when we accept ourselves for what we are and cease to pretend."**

The Matrix

Johari's window is a fascinating matrix on the human personality. It consists of four quadrants.

The **first quadrant** consists of those things **you know about you** and **others know about** you. It is your public persona or **image**. It's what everybody knows about you. It's how you present yourself to the world.

The **second quadrant** consists of those things **you know about you** but **others don't know about you**. This is where we hide our **secrets**. It's who you are in **private**. We'll come back to this quadrant.

The **third quadrant** consists of those things **others know about you** but **you don't know about you**. These are our **blindspots**. This is where we need people who will confront us by speaking the truth in love. And this is where we need people who will encourage us by identifying God-given potential we don't see in ourselves.

The **fourth quadrant** consists of those things **you don't know about you** and **others don't know about you**. This is where the Holy Spirit plays a vital role in our lives. It goes back to the logic of Psalm 139. God knows you better than you know you so if you want to get to know yourself you need to get to know God.

Guilty Secrets

The second quadrant is where many of us, to borrow Thoreau's phrase, "**lead quiet lives of desperation**." We hide parts of ourselves because we're afraid that if people really knew us they wouldn't like us. And the more we hide the lonelier we become.

F.W. Boreham said, "**There is nothing in the solar system so isolating as a secret, and especially as a guilty secret. A man with a guilty secret feels lonely in the densest crowd.**"

The English poet John Donne was absolutely brilliant. He went to Oxford when he was eight years-old. I couldn't even spell Oxford when I was eight! He was considered one of the greatest metaphysical poets of all time. He served as dean of St. Paul's cathedral in London. Donne was successful in every sense of the word, but he also lived in a constant state of fear. Here's why: John Donne had a secret. Before his conversion he had written some blasphemous and obscene poetry to the woman he had secretly married. He lived his entire life in constant fear that someone would discover his deep dark secret.

Here's my definition of paradise. **Paradise is having nothing to hide**. Adam and Eve were naked and they knew no shame. They had nothing to hide. But what happened when they ate from the tree of the knowledge of good and evil? They hid from God and they hid from each other. And we've been playing hide-and-seek ever since.

One of our deepest desires is to know and be known. One of our deepest fears is if people really knew us they wouldn't like us. But here is the good news. No one knows you better than God and no one loves you more than God.

The One who knows you the best loves you the most.

That's something you can base your identity on!

The Great Inversion

⊹→══◎═══←⊹

On April 3rd, 1997, an Irish phone company named *Eircom* announced a unique competition. Every town in Ireland with a population under thirty-thousand was eligible to become what Eircom called "The Information Age Town." The prize was a computer and free Internet access for every household in that town. One of the contestants was the sleepy village of Ennis. They coaxed Eircom officials into a helicopter and taught a thousand school age children to march across the football field spelling out the phrase "Information Age Town."

Ennis won the competition and that's where the story gets interesting. According to Michael Lewis, no one in Ennis even knew what the Internet was! They just knew it was something you were supposed to want. Lewis discovered that the older citizens of Ennis had no idea what to do with the computers after they got them. Some of them never even opened the computer boxes while others actually displayed the computers on fireplace mantles like trophies!

The overnight transition from medieval Irish village to Information Age Town had an interesting side effect. Lewis said, "It inverted long-standing relationships between young people and old people." Instead of adults teaching children, children started teaching adults. The same kids who marched across the football field spelling out the phrase "Information Age Town" offered classes on computers and the Internet.

In Matthew 18, **Jesus inverted the long-standing relationship between young people and old people.** And the Great Inversion is on par, in terms of importance, with the Great Commandment and Great Commission.

The disciples asked Jesus, "Who is the greatest in the kingdom of God?" Jesus picked a little child out of the crowd and said, "I tell you the truth, unless you change and become like little children, you will never enter the kingdom of heaven. Therefore, whoever humbles himself like this little child is the greatest in the kingdom of heaven."

Most religious traditions look to the wise old sage as the epitome of spirituality, but Christianity is child-centric. Children are the centerpiece of Jesus' theology. Christians are called to childlikeness.

Sir John Kirk, the 19th century British Naturalist, once said that if he had his way there would always be a little child positioned in the heart of London—perhaps in the precincts of Westminster Abbey or St. Paul's Cathedral. And he said that no one would be allowed to contest a seat in Parliament or become a candidate for public office until he had spent a day with that child and passed an examination in the child's novel methods of thought, feeling, and expression.

When I first read that I thought, "What a fascinating idea." And then I realized that is exactly what Jesus did in Matthew 18. He proverbially positioned a child at the heart of the kingdom of heaven. You can't get in without becoming like a little child. Little children are the gatekeepers of the kingdom.

Far-Side

There is a difference between **childlikeness** and **childishness** so let me make the distinction.

I Corinthians 13:11 says, "When I was a child I thought like a child, I talked like a child, I reasoned like a child. When I became a man, I put childish ways behind me."

The word "childish" means "simple-minded." Oliver Wendell Holmes said there are two types of simplicity. There's simplicity on the **near-side of complexity**. And there's simplicity on the **far-side of complexity**. God calls us to simplicity on the far-side of complexity.

A lot of Christians have settled for simplicity on the near side of complexity. They're unwilling to deal with doubt. They've never wrestled with paradox. They've never been stretched by the tension of opposites. They have near-side faith. Hebrews 6:1 says, "Let us leave the elementary teachings about Christ and go on to maturity."

I Corinthians 14:20 puts it this way, "Stop thinking like children. In regards to evil be infants, but in your thinking be adults."

We need to avoid childishness at all costs, but we're called to childlikeness.

The Child Within

Dr. Seuss said, "**Adults are obsolete children.**" We need to rediscover the child within. That's not just "pop psychology." That's kingdom theology!

Jesus said we can't enter the kingdom of heaven if we don't become like little children so we ought to take it seriously.

One dimension of spiritual growth is a reversal of the aging process. Childlikeness is rediscovering the child within—the person we were before we were pressured by peers or polluted by the harsh realities of life or perverted by sin. It's the person we were before we developed limitations and assumptions, before we had egos and alter egos. **The child within is who we were before the effects of sin.**

At a recent baptism, an NCCer described her conversion to Christ this way. I'll never forget what she said. "Now I'm the person I was as a child—always smiling and laughing." Jesus used the phrase "born again" to describe conversion because it's about starting all over again. It's a new lease on life. In a sense, it's a second childhood.

Unlearning

I think half of spiritual growth is **learning what we don't know**. The other half is **unlearning what we do know**—those **assumptions** and **prejudices** and **limitations** that accumulate and keep us from becoming the people God wants us to be.

Erasmus said, "Not to know certain things is part of knowledge."

There is a dual phrase repeated throughout the Sermon on the Mount. Jesus says, **"You have heard that it was said."** Then he says, **"But I tell you."**

In other words, **you need to unlearn what you've learned**.

"You have heard that it was said, 'Eye for an eye, and tooth for a tooth.' But I tell you do not resist an evil person."

"You have heard that it was said, 'Love your neighbor and hate your enemy.' But I tell you: Love your enemies."

"You have heard that it was said, 'Do not break your oath.' But I tell you, do not swear at all."

It's all about unlearning. Dee Hock says, "The problem is never how to get new, innovative thoughts into your mind, but how to get old ones out."

That's what Jesus was up against. That's why the Pharisees opposed Jesus. They knew their pharisaical laws so well that they couldn't unlearn them. They were prisoners of their cognitive categories.

Big Foot

Psychologists say we are born with two fears: the fear of falling and the fear of loud noises. That means that **every other fear is learned** which means **every other fear can be unlearned**. There are approximately 2,000 classified fears in medical reference books—everything from photophobia (the fear of never looking good in pictures) to uterophobia (the fear of peanut butter sticking to the roof of your mouth).

I John 4:18 says, "There is no fear in love. But perfect love drives out fear."

As we grow in our love relationship with God we unlearn those fears that paralyze us emotionally and relationally and spiritually.

Faith is the process of unlearning our fears.

As a kid I had my share of fears, but Big Foot was at the top of the list. Every night our family would go through the "Walton Family" routine. We'd all be tucked in bed and I'd say, "Goodnight Mom, goodnight Dad, goodnight Don." My mom and dad would say, "Goodnight Mark, goodnight Don." And my older-brother, Don, would say, "Goodnight Mom, goodnight Dad, goodnight Mark, goodnight Big Foot."

Scared me to death!

My parents would come in for a "Big Foot check" under the bed and in the closet. They would proclaim my room "Big Foot free," but I was still scared stiff. I obeyed the three "fear rules" every child knows instinctively. Get as much of your body under the covers as possible; don't move a muscle; and of course, never ever let any part of your body hang off the edge of the bed because it might not be there in the morning!

In retrospect, I realize my fear was irrational. If Big Foot could have fit under my child-sized bed or in my tiny closet, he really wasn't that big after all. He was Little Foot.

Irrational fears cause far too much sleep-loss! **Is anything more irrational than believing that God can't do anything?**

Our confidence is the byproduct of God's ability to keep his promises. It all comes back to the process of spiritual maturity. It's not about us proving ourselves to God. It's about God proving himself to us over and over again until we have faith in his faithfulness.

God often brings us face-to-face with our fears and then helps us overcome them.

Fear Factor

The phrase **"fear not"** is the most repeated phrase in Scripture. It's repeated 366 times—one time for every day of the year including leap year!

The significance of that is this: God wants you to live by faith and if you're going to live by faith you've got to face your fears.

As a father, my tendency is to overprotect my kids. It seems like I'm constantly saying, "Be careful" to my kids! Part of the reason is that kids are crazy! When Josiah was two years-old he would be halfway down the stairs and fling himself into midair yelling "dada" without me looking! Part of parenting is navigating the fine line between protecting and overprotecting. I've got to help my children face their fears.

God is good at it.

I love the way John Ortberg says it. **"The choice to follow Jesus is the choice for the constant recurrence of fear."** I know some of you are thinking, "Great! So you're saying God is going to scare me."

But consider the alternative. Most of us try to avoid fear, but if you look back on your life you'll discover that **the scariest experiences are often the greatest experiences.**

When I twenty-two years old I went to a week long conference to get my ministerial credentials. I had already met all the educational requirements, but I had to complete this conference to get credentialed.

It was freezing cold that week and people in Illinois have a habit of just leaving their car running when it's freezing cold and they'll only be away from the car for a few minutes. We started pulling pranks by jumping into running cars while no one was looking and moving them a few parking spaces just to play mind games with people. We felt like it was a harmless prank, but here's what we didn't consider. If you see someone jumping into your running car you don't know they're moving it two spaces. You think they're stealing it.

We ended up trying it one too many times. One night I got into a running car, and when I did, someone came sprinting out of the conference center. It was actually an employee at the conference center. I threw the car into park. I jumped out of the car, jumped into the "getaway" car with some friends, and we took off.

The guy actually chased us in his car! I think we topped out at more than 100 mph on those cold, icy roads. It was "pure fear." Probably "pure stupidity" too! But definitely "pure fear." I saw my credentials flash before my eyes!

It was one of the scariest experiences I've ever had, but it's amazing how your perception changes after that kind of experience. You forget how scary it was and you remember how fun it was!

It's tough to describe, but there's something about fear that makes us feel alive.

David Whyte said, "**The price of our vitality is the sum of all our fears.**"

Another way of saying that is this: **the alternative to fear is boredom.**

Faith is the process of unlearning your fears.

The Country of Lost Freshness

⊶⟹⟸⊷

The humility of children is disarming. There is no pride or pretense. There are no inhibitions or hidden agendas. When you're around children you don't need to "put on airs." You can just be yourself.

Jesus said, "Whoever humbles himself like this child is the greatest in the kingdom of heaven." The word "humble" comes from the Greek word *tapeinoo*, which in its strongest form, means "**to humiliate**." No one is better at that than kids!

I remember an incident a few years ago when we had guests over for dinner. My son, Parker, came running through the house yelling "Captain Underpants." And sure enough, all he had on was underpants! Adults don't do that. Why? Because we're self-conscious! But kids don't care what other people think. There is a freedom and innocence that children possess that all of us crave. **But we're so self-conscious we have a hard time experiencing the freedom and innocence of just being ourselves.** We become consumed with thoughts about ourselves. Part of becoming like little children is becoming less self-conscious and more God-conscious.

Wet Feet

If you want to do anything of note for the kingdom of God you've got to be willing to look foolish. You've got to **risk personal humiliation**. You've got to take **childlike chances**.

Faith is the willingness to look foolish.

In Joshua 3, the Lord gives Joshua some interesting instructions. "Tell the priests who carry the Ark of the Covenant: 'When you reach the edge of the Jordan's waters, go and stand in the river'." Then Joshua 3:13 says, "As soon as the priests who carry the ark of the Lord—the Lord of all the earth—set foot in the Jordan, its waters flowing downstream will be cut off and stand up in a heap."

I think we've got it backwards. Most of us want God to part the water before we take a step of faith. But God often requires a step of faith before He'll part the waters!

We read a story like this and it seems like no big deal, but that's because we know the outcome. We've got the box score. I want you to put yourself in the priest's wet shoes. God says he'll part the river, but when was the last time you saw a river parted? Never! My natural reaction would be to say, "God, why don't you part the river and then I'll step into the riverbed." God says, "Why don't you get your feet wet and I'll part the river."

Some people have a God-given dream but it is unfulfilled because they're waiting for God to part the waters while God is waiting for them to get their feet wet.

Joshua 3:15 says that the Jordan river was at flood stage. I'd probably question God's timing. "Maybe we should wait till the floodwaters recede." And ten years later we're still landlubbers watching the tide come in and go out.

If I'm one of the priests I'm thinking, "If God doesn't

part the water I'm going to look awfully foolish with wet feet." But maybe that's the point. Faith is the willingness to look foolish.

Noah looked foolish building an ark in the dessert. Sarah looked foolish buying maternity clothes at ninety-nine. David looked foolish attacking Goliath with a slingshot. Peter looked foolish stepping out of the boat in the middle of the lake in the middle of a storm. Jesus looked foolish hanging half-naked on a cross. But that's faith—a willingness to look foolish. And the results speak for themselves.

Noah was saved from the flood. Sarah gave birth to Isaac. David defeated Goliath. Peter walked on water. And Jesus was raised from the dead.

I Corinthians 1:27 says, "God choose the foolish things of the world to shame the wise."

Faith often feels foolish at the outset. It only makes sense in retrospect. You've got to be willing to endure a little humiliation. But in the end you'll look like a genius.

In 1750, philanthropist Jonas Hanway was the laughing-stock of London. During rainstorms, people would jeer and laugh and mock him. They made fun of him because he was the first man to carry an umbrella. But he was willing to look foolish. Two hundred and fifty years later, it's the people who walk around without umbrellas when it's raining that look foolish!

The willingness to look foolish is the key to progress—spiritual, occupational, relational, and intellectual. Ludwig Wittgenstein said, "If people did not sometimes do silly things, nothing intelligent would ever get done."

The reason some of us never reach the Promise Land is because we aren't willing to look foolish. We'd never verbalize it, but we think to ourselves, "I can't pray for someone to be healed. I might look foolish. I can't share my faith with my friends. I might look foolish. I can't seek out counseling for my issues. I might look foolish. I can't ask her out. I might look foolish. I can't change majors. I might look foolish."

Let me say it like it is: **if you aren't willing to look foolish you're a fool**.

Impossible Odds

There is a pattern that I see repeated throughout Scripture: **sometimes God won't intervene until something is humanly impossible**. I think it reveals part of God's personality. God loves impossible odds. And I can relate to that.

One of the most exhilarating things in the world is doing something that no one thinks you can do. As a kid I turned everything into a competition. I loved a challenge. We'd be driving in the car and I'd say something like, "Do you think I can hold my breath for one mile?" Or we'd be taking a walk and I'd say, "Do you think I can jump three sidewalk squares?" Or we'd be eating dinner and I'd say, "Do you think I can eat this Ice Cream Sundae in thirty seconds?"

If someone said, "Yes," I wouldn't even bother trying! What's the point of doing something that someone thinks you can do? So I'd **up the ante** or **raise the stakes**. "Do you think I can hold my breath for two miles?"

I'd raise the stakes and finally when no one thought it was possible I would attempt the impossible. One of the greatest highs in the world is doing what no one thinks you can do.

God loves impossible odds. He loves doing what is humanly impossible.

I think Erwin McManus is right when he says that God may actually "leverage all odds against you, just so that you know that is wasn't your gifts but His power through your gifts that fulfilled His purpose in your life."

The story of Gideon is a great example.

1,000,000:1

Gideon had an army of 32,000 men and they are vastly outnumbered by the Midianites. Judges 6:5 says it was "impossible to count" them. So the odds are already at least 100:1. Then the Lord says, "You have too many men for me to deliver Midian into their hands." If I'm Gideon I'm thinking God misspoke. "You said 'too many' but what you really meant to say was 'too few'."

The Lord says, "You heard me right. You've got too many men." And He tells Gideon to get rid of anyone who is afraid. Gideon loses two-thirds of his army—22,000 out of 32,000 go home! He's left with ten thousand and the odds are up to 10,000:1.

Then the Lord says in verse 4, "There are still too many men." So God devises a test. Gideon's army goes to get a drink of water and God tells him to get rid of the men who drink like a dog and another 9,700 are eliminated. Gideon is left with an "army" of 300 men. And the odds go up to 1,000,000:1.

And it gets better!

God tells Gideon to attack the Midianites with trumpets and jars! You've got to be kidding me! What kind of battle plan is that? And here's the kicker: Israel wins!

Why does God do it that way? Judges 7:2 tells us why. God defeats the Midianites with 300 Israelites instead of 32,000 Israelites so that "Israel may not boast against me that her own strength has saved her."

If Gideon had attacked with 32,000 and won I'm pretty sure the Israelites would have thanked God for "lending them a hand." God would have gotten partial credit. But that's not what God wants or deserves. God wants and deserves full credit. And **when 300 men defeat an army that is impossible to count with trumpets and jars, God gets all the glory!**

God's Grammar

In John 11, a friend of Jesus named Lazarus gets sick and his sisters, Mary and Martha, send an urgent message to Jesus letting him know. We pick up the story in John 11:4. "When he heard this, Jesus said, 'This sickness will not end in death. No, it is for God's glory so that God's Son may be glorified through it.' Now Jesus loved Martha and her sister and Lazarus; and yet when he heard that Lazarus was sick, he stayed where he was two more days."

You would think that he would drop everything and go help his friend, but he doesn't. Then he says in verse 14, "Lazarus is dead, and **for your sake I am glad that I was not there**, so that you may believe. But let us go to him."

Jesus said, "This sickness will not end in death." But the truth is: Lazarus dies. This used to bother me because it seems like Jesus was wrong. Then I happened to hear a sermon by Charles Crabtree titled *God's Grammar* and I'll never forget one statement: **never put a comma where God puts a period and never put a period where God puts a comma**.

I was putting a period where Jesus puts a comma. Jesus didn't say Lazarus wouldn't die. He said it would end in death. The key word is "end." It doesn't end in death. Lazarus was raised from the dead.

Oswald Chambers said, "**Sometimes it looks like God is missing the mark because we're too short-sighted to see what He's aiming for**."

But that still begs the question: why wait? Why didn't Jesus drop everything, return to Bethany, and keep Lazarus from dying by healing him?

Here is my theory.

Jesus could have run to the rescue. He could have healed Lazarus. But Jesus had been there and done that. Jesus wanted to reveal more of his glory. **And sometimes for God to reveal more of His glory, things have to go from** bad to worse! A situation has to become humanly impossible. And that is exactly what happens. Lazarus has been in the tomb for four days! And Jesus says in verse 14, "Lazarus is dead, and for you sake I am glad that I was not there, so that you may believe."

I think Jesus could have healed Lazarus and the level of faith would have bumped up a notch or two. But when you raise someone who has been dead four days, you're never the same!

I don't think any of us like being in situations that are humanly impossible, but that is how God reveals his glory. **Impossible situations are divine opportunities!**

You can't have a resurrection without a crucifixion. All of us love comebacks, but you can't have a comeback with a setback.

Preventative Faith

John 11:17 says, "On his arrival, Jesus found that Lazarus had already been in the tomb for four days." So Jesus walks back into a situation where Mary and Martha have been mourning for four days and no doubt wondering why Jesus wasn't there!

Let me juxtapose Mary and Martha and notice their different responses. Verse 32 records Mary's reaction. "Lord, if you had been here, my brother would not have died."

Now here is Martha's response in verse 21. She says exactly what Mary says, "Lord, if you had been here, my brother would not have died." But she takes it one step further. She says, "Lord, if you had been here, my brother would not have died. But I know that **even now** God will give you whatever you ask."

I think this passage reveals two different kinds of faith. Mary had what I would call **preventative faith**. There was no doubt in her mind that Jesus could have come and kept Lazarus from dying.

Here's a definition of preventative faith. It is faith is faith in God's ability to prevent something from happening. And preventative faith is great. I pray a "hedge of protection" around my kids all the time. I think a lot of us pray for traveling mercies. There is even a line in the Lord's Prayer, "Lead us not into temptation." Those are preventative prayers. But there is another level of faith beyond preventative faith. I call it die-hard faith.

Die Hard Faith

Martha says, "Lord, if you had been here, my brother would not have died." So she has preventative faith just like Martha. But then she says something that is absolutely astounding. She says, "But I know that even now God will give you whatever you ask."

Die hard faith is faith that God can **reverse the irreversible!** And that is whole different ballgame when it comes to faith.

When I was a sophomore in college, I blew out my knee in the last game of our basketball season. I went to the doctor for a diagnosis and he said I tore my anterior cruciate ligament. I asked him how long it'd take to heal and he said, "Never."

I'll never forget the feeling of finality—the damage was done and there was nothing I could do about it. I learned a lesson the hard way that day: some things in life are irreversible. You can't untear ligaments.

For what it's worth, I've also learned from personal experience that you can't **undelete documents, unbake cookies, uncut hair** or **unrun red lights.** Some things in life are irreversible, but something happened 2,000 years ago that changed the rules of the game. On a Sunday morning, three days after Jesus was crucified, **God reversed the irreversible**.

One of my favorite phrases in Scripture is found in

Romans 4:18. It says, "**Against all hope**, Abraham in hope believed and so became the father of many nations." He could have given up, but it says, "Without weakening in his faith, he faced the fact that his body was as good as dead—since he was about a hundred years old—and that Sarah's womb was also dead."

I love that phrase, "Against all hope." Sarah had stopped ovulating. The natural window of opportunity had closed. You don't reverse the effects of aging. But that is exactly what God does. Abraham and Sarah have a child because they had die-hard faith.

Die hard faith is faith in God's ability to reverse the irreversible. In the case of Abraham and Sarah, it was faith that God would give them a child despite the physical realities.

In the case of Martha, her brother has been dead for four days but she was still holding out hope. That is die hard faith in the most literal sense!

Eternal Optimists

Let me share two personal convictions. John 16:33 says, "In this world you will have trouble. But take heart, I have overcome the world." That one verse is **so full of realism** and **so full of optimism**.

Here are my two convictions. I think, as followers of Christ, **we ought to be the most realistic people on the planet**. Jesus was saying, "Just because you follow me doesn't mean that you are exempt or immune to problems." Faith doesn't mean that we are "out of touch with reality." Romans 4:18 says that Abraham, "**Faced the fact** that is body was as good as dead."

We ought to be the most realistic people on the planet. But we also **ought to be the most optimistic people on the planet**, by virtue of the resurrection! If Jesus can raise the dead then all bets are off! The resurrection totally redefined what is and what is not possible.

The word "overcome" in John 16:33 is the same word that is used in Romans 8:37 where it says we are "more than conquerors." I love the way Oswald Chambers described the ramifications. "No power on earth or in hell can conquer the Spirit of God in a human spirit, it is an **inner unconquerableness**."

We ought to be eternal optimists! And that optimism isn't some life insurance policy that we invoke on our deathbed. It is something that infuses every situation with optimism.

Moving Mountains

Jesus said, "If you have faith as small as a mustard seed, you can say to this mountain, 'Move from here to there' and it will move. **Nothing will be impossible for you**."

The phrase "moving mountains" was a Jewish figure of speech that referred to anything that seemed impossible. Mountains were considered the most stable of all things. They were immovable. So to move a mountain would be the most incomprehensible feat. By stark contrast, a mustard seed was the tiniest of seeds. It was synonymous with "small quantity." Jesus intentionally used two opposite images—the most incomprehensible feat and the smallest conceivable quantity of faith—to make a point. And the point is this: God can take the smallest quantity of faith and accomplish the impossible. A little faith goes a long way!

From a human perspective, there are degrees of difficulty. There are small problems and big problems, small miracles and big miracles. We tend to think of our prayer requests as having different degrees of difficulty. But with God, there is no big or small, easy or difficult, possible or impossible. **To the infinite, all finites are equal**.

As Jeremiah 32:17 says, "Nothing is too difficult for you." There are no degrees of difficulty with God.

Floating Axheads

II Kings 6 records one of my favorite Old Testament stories. "Elisha and a company of prophets went to the Jordan river and began to cut down trees. As one of them was cutting down a tree, the iron axhead feel into the water. 'Oh, my lord,' he cried out, 'it was borrowed.' Elisha asked, 'Where did it fall?' When he showed him the place, Elisha cut a stick and threw it there, and made the iron float. 'Lift it out,' he said. Then the man reached out his hand and took it."

Iron axheads don't float. They sink. Period.

Once it's gone it gone. It reminds of Jack Handey's deep thought, "If you ever drop your keys into a river of molten lava, let 'em go man, cause they're gone."

If I'm Elisha, I try to console the guy. "I'm sorry you lost your axhead." I may even let him use mine or help him find a replacement. But what I love about Elisha is that he doesn't give up. He's seen God do the impossible before and he believes that God can do the impossible again. Elisha throws a stick in the river. The iron axhead floats. Problem solved.

Here's the thing: if Elisha didn't believe God could do it, he would have never tried it. **You have to believe it to achieve it**. To borrow Jesus' words, "You have not because you ask not." God is honored when we ask for the impossible.

The truth is that God does the impossible every day!

You may say, "I've never experienced a miracle."

I beg to differ.

Right now you have no sensation of motion, but you are traveling 66,600 mph through space. Today you will travel more than 1.5 million miles in your annual trek around the sun. Not only that, the earth is rotating on its axis at about 1,000 mph. Now let me ask you a question: **when was the last time you thanked God for keeping us in orbit?** When was the last time you said, "God, I wasn't sure we were going to make the full rotation today. Thanks!"

You already trust God for the big stuff like keeping

the planets in orbit. You just need to trust him with the "little stuff." Randy Hurst says, "God is great not because nothing is too big for him. **God is great because nothing is too small for him.**"

The Country of Lost Freshness

Henry James called the passage of years a slow, reluctant march into enemy country—"the country of lost freshness." James theorized that if a person never lost their freshness they would never grow old.

I find that fascinating in light of Proverbs 29:11. "Without a vision the people perish." The word "perish" means "to rot." **If you don't have a vision there is nothing to stop the process of decay in your life.** You become stale. **Vision is a preservative.** It keeps us from getting old.

Caleb was one of twelve spies who explored the Promise Land and one of two that brought back a positive report. The Israelites didn't listen to Caleb's advice and wandered aimlessly for forty years as a result. Forty-five years later, Caleb is an octogenarian. He says, "Here I am today, eight-five years old! I am still as strong today as the day Moses sent me out: I'm just as vigorous to go out to battle now as I was then."

And then you can hear forty-five years of pent-up conviction in his voice. "Now give me this hill country that the Lord promised me that day." Caleb doesn't want Joshua to give him a settled piece of property. He's not ready to retire! He wants the hill country—the land of giants.

Let me ask you a question: do you know very many people who are as strong and as vigorous at eighty-five as they were at forty-five? How can Caleb be "as strong" and "as vigorous" after wandering in the wilderness for forty years? The answer is simple: the vision of possessing the Promise Land never died. And that vision kept him young.

Harriet Doerr said, "**One of the best things about aging**

is being able to watch imagination overtake memory." She knows where of she speaks. Harriet dreamed of going to college, but money then marriage then kids kept her from going. But the dream never died. Not only did she graduate from Stanford University with a BA. She did it at sixty-seven years of age! And Harriet wasn't about to stop there. She dreamed of writing a book. Her first book, *Stones for Ibarra*, was published when she was seventy-four years old.

Ashley Montague said, **"I want to die young at a ripe old age."**

That's what dreams will do for you! They keep you young.

You start dying when you have nothing worth living for and you start living when you have something worth dying for.

One of my favorite words is neoteny. It's a zoological term that means **"the retention of youthful qualities by adults."** You never lose that childlike wonder. Your sense of possibility never dissipates. You're full of curiosity and energy and playfulness. You get old, but you stay young.

Cicero may have said it best. **"For as I like a young man in whom there is something old, so I like an old man in whom there is something young."**

Act IV: The Goal

❖⇒◎⇐❖

He is no fool who loses what he cannot keep
to gain what he cannot lose

Jim Elliot

Human beings are wired for worship. **All of us worship all the time**. The question isn't whether or not we'll worship. The question is: who will we worship? And you have two choices: you can worship you or you can worship the God who created you. You can build monuments to yourself or you can build altars to God.

Here's the problem with worshipping the god of you: you run out of stuff to worship real quick. You're world gets smaller and smaller until all that's left is little you. Louis Giglio says, "If you give all your praise to the god of you, **you'll become a disappointing little god to both yourself and to all those who trust in you**." You weren't created to worship you. You were created to worship the God who created you.

Psalm 115:1 says, "Not to us, O Lord, not to us but to

your name be the glory."

When we're hitting on all eight cylinders spiritually we're living exclusively for the glory of God. But too often we settle for something less. The theological word is idolatry.

Psalm 115:4 says, "Their idols are silver and gold, made by the hands of men. They have mouths, but cannot speak, eyes, but they cannot see; they have ears, but cannot hear, noses, but they cannot smell; they have hands, but cannot feel, feet, but they cannot walk; nor can they utter a sound with their throats."

And here is the prophetic punch line in verse 8. "**Those who make them will be like them.**"

Here's the bottom line: **you become what you worship**. If you don't like who you're becoming you're worshipping the wrong things! **Identity problems are worship problems**. Start worshipping God and you'll become the person God created you to be.

Mice and Monarchs

⊷⇒⊂⊷

F.W. Boreham playfully recalls an interesting incident in one of his writings. A small boy was given the honor of presenting a bouquet of flowers to the Queen of England, but he got down on all fours and starting rummaging around her feet. He explained later that he thought he had seen a mouse! Boreham makes a great observation: **to a child, monarchs and mice are of equal interest.** Children are equally interested in everything.

St. Chrysostom believed the preeminent charm of childhood lay in its scorn of those social distinctions that enslave us later in life. **We become prisoners of our own presuppositions and prejudices.**

Ellen Langer calls them **"premeditated cognitive commitments"** in her book *Mindfulness.* If you're skeptical or critical, you're going to find something to be skeptical or critical about. A pessimist will always see something bad in a good situation and an optimist will always see something good in a bad situation. Why? **Because we tend to see what we're looking for!**

Reticular Activating System

There is a cluster of nerve cells at the base of your brainstem that form the reticular activating system (RAS). You are constantly bombarded by countless stimuli—sights and sounds and smells. The RAS serves as a filter. It's the brain's radar system. It determines what gets noticed and what goes unnoticed.

If you buy a new car, you will suddenly notice that same kind of car everyplace you go. That's a function of the reticular activating system. It's not like everyone went out and bought the same car at the same time you did. It's the simple fact that when you bought the car, a category was created by your reticular activating system. You now notice what went unnoticed. It registers on your radar.

The Apostle Paul gives us a list of eight "premeditated cognitive commitments" in Philippians 4. He says, "Whatever is true, whatever is noble, whatever is right, whatever is pure, whatever is lovely, whatever is admirable—if anything is excellent or praiseworthy—think about such things."

If you're looking for those things you'll find them. If you aren't you won't.

A few years ago I kept a gratitude journal. It was inspired by Psalm 100:2. "Forget not all His benefits." Everyday I journaled three things I was grateful for. As I look back on that season of my life, I realize that I've never been more grateful. And it's not rocket science. If you're looking for things to be grateful for you're going to find things to be grateful for. That gratitude journal created a category in my RAS. No matter how bad a day I had, my RAS knew I needed to find three things each day to be grateful for!

Mindfulness

Ellen Langer says, "Mindlessness sets in when we rely too rigidly on categories created in the past." We need to create new categories. Jesus called them new "wine skins." Langer says, "**Just as mindlessness is the rigid reliance on old categories, mindfulness means the continual creation of new ones.**"

Proverbs 18:15 says, "The intelligent man is always open to new ideas."

I love the way Gandhi said it. "**Live as if you were to die tomorrow. Learn as if you were to live forever.**"

Part of becoming like little children is the continual creation of new mental categories.

The word "education" means to "**draw out.**" But if you walked into the average classroom you'd think that education means "to cram in."

Several centuries ago, Plato said, "Do not train youths to learn by force and harshness, but direct them to it by what amuses their minds so that you may be better able to discover with accuracy the peculiar bent of the genius of each."

Proverbs 22:6 is a protocol for parenting. It says, "Train a child in the way he should go, and when he is old he will not depart from it."

Parents must become students of their children. One of the primary goals of parenting is self-discovery. Parents help their children discover who God has created them to be. We need to instill values, but the goal is not domestication. The goal is to unleash our children so that they live in reckless abandon to God. Part of parenting is staying out of the way and allowing our children to be children. We live in a culture where children grow up too fast. Instead of encouraging children to become like adults we need to encourage adults to become like children.

Questions

According to the research of Rolf Smith, kids ask 125 probing questions every day. Adults ask six. That means that **somewhere between childhood and adulthood we**

lose 119 questions per day! Somewhere along the way, adults lose that childlike curiosity.

Those of you who have children resonate with this research. And kids don't ask garden-variety questions. They probe the deepest philosophical issues of the universe. Every question seems to be a brainteaser. And the more questions your kids ask the dumber you feel. Every day, there is the very real possibility that you're going to feel like a complete idiot because you can't answer their easiest questions!

A few years ago I did a little experiment. I kept track of the questions my then five-year old son, Parker, was asking me. Here is a small sampling.

Where do hills live?

Why do whales live in water?

Why do planes go over cars?

Why do caterpillars turn into butterflies?

Why do stars only come out at night?

Why do houses have doors?

Why do horses bounce?

I said, "You mean trot?" He said, "No, I mean bounce!"

I made the fatal mistake of trying to turn the tables. I wanted Parker to understand that there's not an easy answer to every question. So I thought I'd pull out a stumper. I gave Parker a little of his own medicine. I said, "Parker, why does it rain?" Without a moment's hesitation, he replied, "Because everything is thirsty." You had to hear it. The tone of his voice sounded like he wanted to put his arm around my shoulder and say, "Dad, let me explain to you the mysteries of the universe."

The most-repeated word in a child's vocabulary is "why." Kids ask endless questions because kids are curious.

Synaptogenesis

According to the research of Dr. Peter Huttenlocher, the synapses in babies' brains form at the incredible rate of up to three billion per second. Between birth and eight months, the synaptic connections in babies' brains skyrocket from fifty trillion to one quadrillion. Almost like the telephone wires that crisscross a metropolitan area, the brain is being hardwired for life.

Dr. Harry Chugani, the pediatric neurologist who pioneered PET scans, compares the active brain to a nuclear reaction. There are millions of neurons firing across billions of neural pathways every second of every day. According to Dr. Chugani, a child's brain pulsates at about 225 times the rate of the average adult. If you're a parent, that explains a lot!

The brain is roughly the size of a softball. It only weighs three pounds. Yet neurologists estimate that **we have the capacity to learn something new every second of every minute of every hour of every day for the next 300 million years!**

Dr. Peter Anokin of Moscow University concluded a 60-year study of the human mind with these words, "We can show that each of the ten billion neurons in the human brain has a possibility of connections of one with twenty-eight noughts (zeroes) after it! If a single neuron has this quantity of potential, we can hardly imagine what the whole brain can do. What it means is that the total number of possible combinations/permutations in the brain, if written out, would be 1 followed by 10.5 million kilometers of noughts!"

The bottom line is that we have not used 1/100th of 1%

of our brain's potential.

What does that have to do with discipleship?

The word disciple comes from the Greek word *mathetes* which means "learner."

By definition, **a disciple is someone who never stops learning**. Learning is not a luxury. Learning is a stewardship issue. It is making the most of the mind God has given us. The ancient philosopher Seneca said, "Nothing is more dishonorable than an old man, heavy with years, who has no evidence of having lived long except his age."

The most important law of ecology is this: $L > C$. For an organism to survive, the rate of learning (L) must be equal to or greater than the rate of change (C). In his book *Megatrends 2000*, John Naisbitt says, "Learning how to learn is what it's all about." Alvin Toffler adds, "The illiterate of the future are not those who cannot read or write, but those who cannot learn, unlearn, and relearn."

Curiosity is part of the image of God. Curiosity is what fuels the human spirit to discover creation and the Creator.

Ologies

I love to read. Pre-college I rarely picked up a book that wasn't assigned. Post-college I've read on average 150-200 books a year. I'm interested in everything. I love studying other ologies—biology, psychology, neurology. Here's my worldview in a nutshell: **all "ologies" are branches of theology**. I don't want that to sound pejorative, but learning about what God has made is one way of learning about God. We learn about the creator by studying creation. That's what Romans 1:20 says. Nature reveals God's "invisible qualities." Gary Thomas says, "Any study that explores, examines, and explains the natural world can shed some light on the nature of our God and help us know him better."

I split my undergrad education between the University of Chicago and Central Bible College. When I was at CBC I took a lot of classes in theology and they helped shape my worldview. But if you were to ask me what class had the greatest theological impact on me, I would have to say it was a class on immunology at the University of Chicago hospital center. The professor never mentioned God. But the entire course was an exposition of Psalm 139:14 where David said, "I praise you because I am fearfully and wonderfully made."

Every class I walked away with a greater appreciation of how fearfully and wonderfully we're made. And I had the same reaction as David. He said, "I praise you." I would walk away from the classes wondering how anyone could doubt the existence of an intelligent designer.

The arts and sciences—everything from psychology to physics to history to musicology—are attempts to understand creation. And all attempts to understand creation reveal something about the Creator.

Proverbs 25:2 says, "It is the glory of God to conceal a matter; to search out a matter is the glory of kings."

It is almost like a cosmic game of cat and mouse or hide-and-seek.

Francis Bacon had a fascinating take on that verse. He said, "Solomon, although he excelled in the glory of treasure and magnificent buildings, of shipping and navigation, of fame and renown, yet he maketh no claim to any of those glories, but only to the glory of inquisition of truth; for so he saith, 'The glory of God is to conceal a thing, but the glory of the king is to find it out!'; as if, according to the innocent play of children, the Divine Majesty took delight to hide his works, in the end to have them found out; and **as if kings could not obtain a greater honour than to be God's playfellows in that game.**"

Terra Incognita

Genesis 1:28 is humankind's **original job description.** "God blessed them and said to them, 'Be fruitful and increase in number; fill the earth and subdue it. Rule over the fish of the sea and birds of the air and over every living creature that moves on the ground."

On the edge of medieval maps, cartographers inscribed two Latin words—*terra incognita*. Everything beyond the edge of those maps was unknown territory.

In the beginning, everything outside Eden was *terra incognita*. And God invites Adam and Eve to explore. We assume that if Adam and Eve hadn't eaten from the tree of knowledge of good and evil they would have stayed in the Garden of Eden forever, but that was never God's game plan. Long before Adam and Eve were banished from the garden, God said, "Fill the earth." It was an invitation to explore!

Planet Earth was untamed, uninhabited, undiscovered. They could travel 24,859 miles in any direction and discover mountains and deserts and jungles and oceans. There were 196,949,970 square miles of *terra incognita*.

Not unlike Columbus who was commissioned by the King and Queen of Spain to discover a westward route to the Indies; not unlike Lewis and Clark who were commissioned by President Jefferson to explore the newly acquired Louisiana Purchase; and not unlike Sir Francis Drake who was commissioned by the Queen of England to circumnavigate the globe; Adam and Eve were commissioned by God to explore planet Earth.

I don't know if you've ever thought about that phrase in those terms, but the invitation to explore is a divine calling. **One way we glorify God is by exploring what He's made and praising Him in the process**.

Just as an artist or composer wants others to enjoy his art or music, God wants us to enjoy His creation. He wants us to explore it, to study it, to name it, to admire its beauty.

Exploration honors God.

The astronomer who charts galaxies billions of light-years away; the geneticist who maps the human genome; the researcher who seeks a cure for Parkinson's disease; the oceanographer who explores the ocean floor; the ornithologist who studies and preserves rare bird species; the physicist who tries to catch quarks; the chemist who charts molecular structures; and the theologian who studies God have one things in common. All of them are explorers. They are fulfilling humankind's original job description.

If that doesn't sound spiritual, your definition of spirituality needs to be super-sized.

D4DR

A few years ago I read an article in *Time Magazine* devoted to the rise in popularity of adventure sports. It said, "America has embarked on a national orgy of thrill seeking and risk taking."

One snapshot captures base jumper, Mark Lichte, riding his bicycle off a 3,000 foot cliff in Norway. That's what base jumpers do. They ride their bikes off cliffs and plummet hundreds of feet before deploying their parachutes. Base jumping has one of the sporting world's highest fatality rates. The compelling question is: why would anyone in their right mind would risk death by riding a bike off a cliff?

Israeli researchers may have found the answer—a strand of DNA known as *D4DR*. Researchers call it **the thrill-seeking gene**. We are genetically wired for adventure. Jonathan Senk says, "It's the Lewis and Clark gene, to venture out, to find what your limitations are."

Helen Keller said, **"Life is either a daring adventure or it is nothing."**

We crave adventure.

I recently chaperoned a fieldtrip for Summer's first-grade class. I don't know if you're ever been around twenty-five first graders on a fieldtrip, but if you could somehow bottle the energy I think you could power a small country!

I looked back at one point and all I saw was twenty-five

heads bouncing up and down. It was like ping pong balls in a lottery machine! The kids were yelling and laughing and jumping up and down in their seats.

We ended up going to the *Navy Memorial*. The funny thing is that everybody, including the teacher, thought we were going to the *Navy Yard*. There is a difference.

So we didn't know where we were going or what we were doing once we got there. But these kids could care less. We could have stayed on that bus for four hours and the kids would have loved it.

At one point I had this thought: if these kids are this excited about a fieldtrip and they don't even know where they're going or what they're doing once they get there, **we ought to be bouncing off the walls at the thought of heaven**. You want to talk about a fieldtrip!

It ought to consume our thoughts. It ought to make our hearts skip a beat. It ought to fill us with unadulterated, unbridled anticipation. But I don't think it does. I think the average first-grader gets more excited about a fieldtrip to nowhere than we get about our eternal fieldtrip to heaven. And my question is why? I think the answer is pretty simple. We don't talk about heaven. We don't think about heaven. So we don't have a vision of heaven.

Proverbs 23:7 says, "As a man thinketh in his heart, so is he" (*KJV*). In other words, your thought life reveals who you really are. You are what you think about. Let me extrapolate and take that principle one step further: **whatever you think about the most is the most important thing to you and the most important thing about you**.

Who you are is shaped by what you think about. James Allen said, "A noble and Godlike character is not a thing of favor or chance, but is the natural result of continued effort in right thinking, the effect of long-cherished association with Godlike thoughts."

So much of spiritual development comes back to the

answer to this very simple question: **how much do you think about God?**

There's an old aphorism that some people are "too heavenly minded to be any earthly good." I understand the train of thought, but the opposite is true. The more heavenly minded we are the more earthly good we'll be.

Peter Kreeft makes a profound observation. "Our pictures of Heaven simply do not move us; they are not moving pictures. It is this aesthetic failure rather than intellectual or moral failures in our pictures of Heaven and of God that threatens faith most potently today. Our pictures of Heaven are dull, platitudinous and syrupy; therefore, so is our faith, our hope, and our love of Heaven. It doesn't matter whether it's a dull life or a dull truth. **Dullness, not doubt, is the strongest enemy of faith.**"

The rapture is going to be the ultimate adrenaline rush! And heaven is going to be an endless adventure. According to the latest astronomical estimates, there are approximately 80 billion galaxies. That is about 10 galaxies per person! I don't think we'll run out of things to do. The six billion people on this planet have barely explored one planet in one galaxy!

Brent Curtis said, "**He who has been faithful in the small things will be given even greater adventures in heaven.** We long for adventure, to be caught up in something larger than ourselves, a drama of heroic proportions. This isn't just a need for continual excitement; it's part of our design. **Part of the adventure will be to explore the wonders of the new heaven and new earth, the most breathtaking of which will be God himself.** We will have all eternity to explore the mysteries of God, and not just explore, but celebrate and share with one another."

The Law of Fascination

Jeremiah 2:19 says, "I remember the devotion of your youth, how as a bride you loved me." Jeremiah is describing the spiritual honeymoon that all of us experience when we come into relationship with Christ. But somewhere along the way something happens to Israel. Jeremiah 2:19 says, **"You have lost the awe of me."**

A.W. Tozer talks about what he calls the law of fascination. Fascination is to be spellbound by some irresistible charm. If something doesn't fascinate us we can take it or leave it. Tozer said, **"Christians who do not know this law will never be anything but half-Christians all their lives."**

To live in awe of God is to be spellbound by God. He is the supreme fascination. He is the object of our curiosity.

Our family went to see David Copperfield not long ago. Parker and Summer were going through a "magic phase" so I knew they'd love the show. Throughout the performance, Summer kept leaning over and saying, "Dad, how did he do that?" I kept saying, "I have no idea!"

During his final act he made ten randomly selected people disappear. It was absolutely spellbinding, but that wasn't the best part of the show. In fact, it wasn't anything David Copperfield did. **The best part of the show was the expressions on the faces of my children.** They watched the show in wide-eyed wonder! The look on their faces was priceless.

Luke 11:33 says, **"Live in wide-eyed wonder"** (*The Message*).

To be filled with the Spirit is to be filled with wonder. I love the way one Greek Orthodox theologian put it. **"It is not the task of Christianity to provide easy answers to every question,** but to make us progressively aware of mystery. God is not so much the **object of our knowledge** as the **cause of our wonder."**

The Neurology of Christianity

⊷⊜⊷

Study is a spiritual discipline. I love to study creation and the Creator, but up until a few years ago I felt like it was somehow less spiritual than praying or fasting or worshipping. Then I came across an aphorism in the *Talmud*, the Jewish commentary on the Old Testament. It said, "**An hour of study is as an hour of prayer.**"

That one insight proved to be a paradigm shift.

II Timothy 2:15 says, "Study to show thyself approved unto God, a workman that needeth not be ashamed, rightly dividing the word of truth" (*KJV*). **Study is a form of worship.** One way we worship God is by "doing our homework." Too often there is a disconnect between the spiritual and intellectual.

Webster defines "intellectual" as "given to study, reflection, and speculation." Intellectuals aren't necessarily intelligent. They just love to learn. When I discover something new about God it makes me want to worship. If I'm not learning anything new about God I feel spiritually stagnant. In the words of Madeleine L'Engle, "I need questions that do not have answers."

All of us have different spiritual temperaments. Study is to the intellectual type what singing is to the musical type.

At Odds

One of the greatest mistakes we can make is thinking that the intellectual and spiritual parts of us are enemies instead of allies. I don't think you can be intellectual, in the truest sense of the word, without being spiritual. And I don't think you can be spiritual, in the truest sense of the word, without being intellectual.

Let me explain.

John 4:24 says that the Father is seeking worshippers who will worship him "in spirit and in truth." There is a spiritual element and an intellectual element. Let me go out on a limb. The intellectual has the greatest potential to worship God. It's pretty simple: **the more you know about God the more you can worship him**.

Learning and worshipping are not mutually exclusive things. In fact, they are directly proportional. The more you know the more you can worship. I can worship God more now than I could five years ago because I know Him better.

In this book, *Mozart's Brain and the Fighter Pilot*, author Richard Restak says, "The richer my knowledge of flora and fauna of the woods, the more I'll be able to see. Our perceptions take on richness and depth as a result of all the things that we learn. What the eye sees is determined by what the brain has learned. This suggests a short mantra: **learn more, see more**." In a sense, learning gives us depth perception.

Think about it in these terms. When an astronomer looks into the night sky, they have a greater appreciation for the heavens because they **see more**. They know the constellations by name. When a musician listens to a concerto, they have a greater appreciation because they **hear more**. They know the notes that are being played.

In her book, *Unwinding the Clock*, Bodil Jonsson makes a great observation about life. She says, "Once upon a time I thought that getting older would be like moving down a narrowing funnel—life would just get more constricted." But she says, "It seems quite the opposite." Here is how she explains it. "It's like the biologist who can distinguish hundreds of different types of grass while other people see green and more green. The experience of experts are richer than those of other people."

All worship is not equal. **The more you know the more you can worship**. The intellectual and spiritual parts of us are intimately interconnected. Studying and worshipping aren't at odds with each other. They are one and the same pursuit.

Ignorance Isn't Bliss

Think of truth as a spectrum: on one side is **ignorance** and on the other side is **knowledge**. Now listen to what Jesus says in John 4:22. "You Samaritans worship what you do not know." In other words, your worship is meaningless because you're worshipping out of ignorance. God doesn't just want you to worship Him. **He wants you to know why you're worshipping Him**!

When Lora and I get into an argument—hypothetically speaking of course—I'll occasionally try to bail out by saying, "Sorry!" I call it a pre-mature apology. And to be perfectly honest, it's a little disingenuous because I'm not sure why I'm sorry or what I'm sorry about. I'm just being too lazy to work through the issue or the problem. Every once in a while Lora will ask the question that strikes fear in every man's heart. "Why are you sorry?" And I have no idea why I'm sorry. And when you don't know why you're sorry it's an empty apology.

Worship without knowledge is empty worship. It's

like you're worshipping God and if God asked, "Why?" you wouldn't know what to say because you aren't sure why you're worshipping or you're worshipping for the wrong reasons. It's like someone saying "thank you" but they don't know why or what for.

God wants to be worshipped "in spirit and in truth." Here's a personal conviction: **our ability to worship is only limited by our knowledge of God**.

In Acts 17:11, Luke commends the Bereans. "Now the Bereans were of more noble character than the Thessalonians, for they received the message with great eagerness and examined the Scriptures to see if what Paul said was true."

Let me make two observations.

The Bereans received the message with "great eagerness." Let me just say it like it is: the average person sitting in the pew will get out of a message what they want to get out of a message. **What you learn will be determined by your attitude going into it**. If you listen with a critical spirit you'll find plenty to be critical of. If you are hungry to learn you're going to learn no matter what is said. The Bereans set the example: they couldn't wait to hear what God was going to say to them through the Paul's teaching.

And then it says they "examined the Scriptures to see if what Paul said was true." That tells me a couple things about the Bereans. Scripture was the ultimate authority in their lives. I try to offer a periodic reminder to our congregation: don't take my word for it. I'm not the final authority. Scripture is. And you're called to study to show yourself approved.

All of us know Christians who crossed the line twenty-five years ago, but they don't have twenty-five years of experience. They have one year of experience repeated twenty-five times. They aren't learning the lessons God is trying to teach them. And God won't graduate us to the second grade if we don't learn what He's teaching in the first grade. He won't set us up for failure so we're held back year after year.

The reason many of us are held back is because **we're so anxious to get out of tough situations that we don't get anything out of tough situations**. We pray, "Get me out of this." We ought to ask, "What are you trying to teach me through this?"

The Mind of Christ

It's good to learn something about everything. It broadens our mind. It's good to learn everything about something. It deepens our mind. But learning is not an end in itself.

II Timothy 3:7 describes the "learning trap" that many people fall into. Paul says, "They are always learning but never able to acknowledge the truth." The goal of learning is not knowledge. The goal of learning is the truth. The goal of learning is not a mind full of factoids. The goal of learning is to think like Christ. Philippians 2:6 says, "Let this mind be in your which was also in Christ Jesus." That is the end goal.

How do we do that?

The answer is found in Colossians 3:16. **"Let the word of Christ dwell in you richly."**

When we read Scripture we download God's operating system. It reconfigures our mind. We stop thinking human thoughts and start thinking God thoughts. Just as a computer's hard drive needs to be defragmented to optimize performance, the mind needs to be defragmented. That happens as we study and apply God's Word to our lives. Romans 12:2 says, "Do not be conformed any longer to the pattern of this world, but be transformed by the renewing of your mind."

Doctors Avi Karni and Leslie Underleider of the National Institutes of Mental Health did a fascinating study a few years ago. They asked subjects to perform a simple motor task—a finger-tapping exercise. As subjects tapped, the doctors conducted an MRI brain scan to identify what part of the brain was being activated. The subjects then practiced the finger exercise daily for four weeks. At the end of the four-week period the brain scan was repeated. In each instance, it revealed that the area of the brain involved in the task had expanded. That simple task—a finger-tapping exercise—literally recruited new nerve cells and rewired neuronal connections.

When we read Scripture our brain is literally rewired. Scripture literally reroutes neuronal connections in the brain. New connections are made. The connections begin to line up with Scripture. Our mind is gradually reconfigured into the mind of Christ.

Split-Brain Believers

Mathematically speaking, **the Great Commandment is twenty-five percent intellectual**. The mind is one of four dimensions of love referenced by Jesus in Matthew 22:37. "Love the Lord your God with all your heart and soul and mind and strength."

In the 1970s, Nobel-prize winner Roger Sperry pioneered split-brain research. His work with epileptic patients revealed that the right and left hemispheres of the brain serve very different cognitive functions. The left-brain is linear and logical. It is responsible for everything from mathematics to linguistics. Without it, life would be **chaotic**. The left-brain is the rational side of us.

The right-brain is intuitive and creative. It is responsible for everything from humor to poetry. Without it, life would be **robotic**. The right-brain is the emotional side of us.

In between the right and left hemispheres is a cluster of neurons called the corpus callosum. It serves as our "dual-processor." It allows us to access both sides of the brain. For what it's worth, women have about 40% more corpus callosum than men which may be the neurological explanation for "a woman's intuition." But don't feel bad guys. You have 20% more bone density!

Loving God with all your mind means loving Him with both hemispheres of your brain—your right-brain and left-brain. It includes the rational and emotional parts. It includes the logical and creative parts. It even includes the humorous part.

The Neurology of Laughter

A recent article in *Discover* magazine documented the discovery of what is considered the holy grail of humor. Using magnetic resonance imaging, neurologists have identified the medial ventral prefrontal cortex as the "seat of humor."

Humor is a complex cognitive process. Neuropsychologists Vinod Goel and Raymond Dolan define humor as "a cognitive juxtaposition of mental sets."

Makes you want to laugh doesn't it?

This may sound strange, but **have you ever told God a joke**? I'm serious. Does loving God with all your mind include the medial ventral prefrontal cortex? I know there's a fine line where we can cross over into sacrilegious territory, but this isn't it. Humor is not just healthy, it's holy. It's a gift from God. God is the one who created us with the capacity to guffaw. Permission to speak frankly? **I don't want a relationship with someone I can't laugh with**.

Maybe God would like to share a laugh with us now and then? Too many people mistakenly see God as a cosmic kill-joy. He is anything but. I think we underestimate God's sense of humor just like we underestimate His power and glory and goodness.

My kids crack me up all the time and I only have three of them! What with six billion of us running around this planet, **I wonder if God ever stops laughing**! There has to be millions of hilarious things happening all the time!

Holy Curiosity

Albert Einstein said, "The important thing is not to stop questioning. Curiosity has its own reason for existing. One cannot help but be in awe when he contemplates the mysteries of eternity, of life, of the marvelous structure of reality. It is enough if one tries merely to comprehend a little of this mystery every day. **Never lose a holy curiosity.**"

Curiosity is an expression of humility. It is recognition that we've got a lot left to learn. I have a catch phrase that I say frequently. "As soon as I'm omniscient I'll let you know." It's an admission of ignorance.

At the end of *The Count of Monte Cristo,* Edmond Dantes writes a letter and he says of himself, "Pray for a man, who, like Satan, momentarily thought himself the equal of God and who, with all the humility of a Christian, came to realize that in God's hands alone reside supreme power and infinite wisdom."

In the philosophy of science there is a concept known as critical realism. It is an admission that we don't know everything there is to know. Russell Stannard says, **"We can never expect at any stage to be absolutely certain that our scientific theories are correct and will never need further amendment."**

We need a degree of critical realism when it comes to faith.

I Corinthians 8:2 captures one dimension of spiritual growth. "The man who thinks he knows something does not yet know as he ought to know." In other words, **the more you know the more you know how much you don't know.** Intellectual humility is a byproduct of spiritual maturity. The longer I walk with Christ the fewer theories I have about God and the more trust I have in God.

Brian McLaren says, **"My faith isn't perfect and it**

isn't static. It is guaranteed by my finitude to be incomplete, inaccurate in many places, out of proportion, in need of continuing midcourse corrections. Therefore, it deserves to be doubted at times—doubted so that it can be corrected. If I didn't doubt my faith, I would protect it, not correct it; defend it, not amend it. **Doubting my faith can be an opportunity for increased faith in God**."

Then McLaren makes a great distinction. He says, "There is a difference—subtle yet very significant—between having faith in my faith and having faith in God."

Having faith in my faith is having faith in my own understanding. Having faith in God is believing that God is beyond my ability to comprehend. He doesn't fit within the confines of the cerebral cortex.

Fully yielding to the sovereignty and incomprehensibility of God is a quantum leap in the journey toward spiritual maturity.

Humility is the willingness to let God be God.

Second-Hand Faith

T.S. Eliot said, "We shall not cease from exploration, and the end of all our exploring, will be to arrive where we started and know the place for the first time."

When I went to the University of Chicago as an eighteen-year-old it was like a lamb being thrown to the intellectual lions. My faith came under attack. Here is how I would describe my first year of college. I went into my freshman year knowing **what I believed**. I ended my freshman year knowing **why I believed what I believed**.

When my faith came under attack I had to do some soul searching. For the first time in my life, a second-hand faith wasn't good enough. I needed to know why I believed what I believed.

Brian McLaren says, "**One way or another, we outgrow the faith of our childhood or youth**. Now we're seeking a faith that we can hold with adult integrity, clear intelligence, and honest feeling." He says, "**Losing the faith that my parents and church had tried to give me was necessary, because I had to find a faith with my own name on it, not just theirs.**"

There is a world of difference between "first-hand" and "second-hand" faith.

Second-hand faith is believing what someone else believes. It's hand-me-down faith. I want to hand off my faith to my kids. And a godly heritage is a great thing, but at some point in their spiritual journey they have to **internalize it** and **personalize it**. It has to become part of who they are—part of the warp and woof of their identity.

If you grew up in church, one of the greatest challenges you face is making the transition from second-hand to first-hand faith.

John 4 documents the process of internalization. A Samaritan woman shares her new found faith and John 4:39 says, "Many of the Samaritans from that town **believed in him because of the woman's testimony.**" That is second-hand faith. Then they have a personal encounter with Jesus. And John 4:42 says, "**We no longer believe just because of what you said**; now we have **heard for ourselves**, and we know that Jesus is the Savior of the world." That is first-hand faith.

As a parent, I don't want my kids to believe because I believe. I want them to believe because they believe. If anything scares me it is my children growing up and walking away from the faith because it was my faith and not their faith. They have to go through the same process of internalization or personalization that I went through.

Cognitive Dissonance

At some point in our spiritual journey we run into something called reality—usually at sixty mph. **Simple answers**

don't work and God doesn't fit into nice, neat boxes. The psychological term is cognitive dissonance. It means "psychological conflict resulting from incongruous beliefs." In other words, **something happens that doesn't jive with what you believe.**

You don't believe in miracles and then a miracle happens. Or a prayer doesn't get answered the way you wanted it to. You've written off Christians as hypocritical and then you meet someone who is genuinely authentic. Or you are disillusioned by a negative church experience. Something happens that conflicts with your beliefs and God doesn't fit into nice neat boxes anymore.

Dissonance comes in two primary flavors: **unanswerable questions** and **unexplainable experiences.**

I never cease to be amazed at the way **two people can experience the same tragedy and one person becomes bitter and the other person becomes better.** One person develops a critical spirit and shrivels up spiritually. It's almost like bitterness slowly poisons them to death! Someone else can go through the same exact circumstances and become a better person because of it.

Ten years ago I directed a parachurch ministry that took a training program for ministry into the inner-city for those who couldn't get out to get an education. One of my first students was a man from Nigeria named Charles who in his sixties. He walked with a cane because he had suffered several stokes that effected his speech and motor skills. I had to help him up and down stairs. Sometimes I would give him a ride home from classes and I had to physically lift his leg out of the car so he could get out.

One day I picked him up from the public housing tenement where he was living and I'll never forget the hat he was wearing. Maybe it was the juxtaposition that struck me. He could hardly walk. He could hardly talk. He lived in public housing. But he was wearing a hat that said, "**God is good.**"

I remember being so convicted and so impacted. Many people going through similar circumstances would have become bitter. But Charles is one of the most upbeat people I've ever met. He has a sweet spirit and a kind heart. Tragedy has made him better, not bitter!

Job 1:20 says, "Job stood up and tore his robe in grief. Then he shaved his head and fell to the ground in worship." Then Job says something so powerful. It's so easy for us to read these words ex post facto. But it had to be so hard for Job to actually say them on the heels of tragedy. "Naked I came from my mother's womb, and naked will I depart. **The Lord has given and the Lord has taken away; blessed be the name of the Lord.**" Job 1:22 says, "Job did not sin by blaming God."

When our lives run into unanswerable questions and unexplainable experiences it can shake our confidence. The compass starts spinning. You lose your bearings and it's easy to walk away from God because you're not sure where He is.

Rediscovering your faith is a process. Brian McLaren talks about his process in *Finding Faith*. "At first I was eighty-percent no, and twenty-percent yes; then it was fifty/fifty for a while, and eventually, **the yes part overshadowed the no part.**"

What a great description of the process of finding faith. Maybe you're 20/80 or 80/20.

McLaren says, "**In your own way and in your own time say to God that one, life-changing word, yes.**"

Hardwired

I read *The Bourne Identity* a few years ago. Jason Bourne is trying to discover who he is. One line is profound. Jason Bourne says, **"I'm a reproduced illusion**." To one degree or another, all of us are reproduced illusions.

The Irish Philosopher, George Berkeley, said it this way. **"To be is to be perceived**." Our perception of ourselves is based on others perception of us.

In his book *Invisible Imprint*, Richard Dobbins says, "Small children do not become who they think they are. **They become who they think other people think they are**." It's called "the looking-glass self."

Dobbins says, "Young children believe everything adults say about them to be absolutely true." I think that why Jesus was so harsh with those who mistreat children or lead them astray.

We were in a McDonald's not too long ago and it had one of those curvy mirrors in the play land. Depending on the angle, those mirrors can make you look tall or short, fat or thin. The mirror distorted the way I saw myself.

In the same way, **the people in our lives are distorted mirrors**. They can magnify or minimize our imperfections. They can make us look better than we are or worse than we are.

We all grow up in a house or mirrors.

No matter how well meaning, your friends and family are distorted mirrors. God is the only mirror that will give you an accurate assessment of who you are.

Romans 12:3 says, "The only accurate way to understand ourselves is by who God is and what God does."

Let me try to say it as concisely as I can: **if you base your identity on the opinions of other people you're worshiping their opinions.**

God's opinion is the only opinion that counts.

Idolatry

Psalm 115:1 says, "Not to us, O Lord, not to us but to your name be the glory."

When we're hitting on all eight cylinders spiritually we're living exclusively for the glory of God. The *Westminster Catechism* says **the chief end of man is to glorify God and enjoy Him forever.** I love John Piper's take. He said, **"God is most glorified in us when we are most satisfied in Him."** But all too often we settle for something less. The technical term is idolatry.

Psalm 115:4 says, "Their idols are silver and gold, made by the hands of men. They have mouths, but cannot speak, eyes, but they cannot see; they have ears, but cannot hear, noses, but they cannot smell; they have hands, but cannot feel, feet, but they cannot walk; nor can they utter a sound with their throats."

The Psalmist is saying it like it is: **it's pretty pointless to worship anything less God.**

It is reminiscent of Elijah's showdown with the prophets of Baal. Elijah challenges the 450 prophets of Baal to a showdown. They climb Mount Carmel and Elijah says, "Get two bulls for us." Each side sets up an altar then Elijah says,

"You call on the name of your god, and I will call on the name of the Lord. The god who answers by fire—he is God." The odds are 450:1.

The prophets of Baal start praying and Elijah starts talking smack. "At noon Elijah began to taunt them. 'Shout louder!' he said. 'Surely he is a god! Perhaps he is deep in thought, or busy, or traveling. Maybe he is sleeping and must be awakened.' But Baal never answers.

Then it's Elijah's turn and he doesn't just call down fire. He says, "Fill four large jars with water and pour it on the offering and on the wood." He does it three times! He makes sure the sacrifice is soaking wet. Then he calls down fire and God answers.

Elijah beats the odds!

Here's the point: it's doesn't matter how many people are praying or how much they pray if they're praying to powerless gods.

A Disappointing Little God

Psalm 115:8 is the punch line. **"Those who make them will be like them."**

Translation: **you become what you worship**.

Louis Giglio says it this way. **"Whatever you value most will ultimately determine who you are.** If you worship money, you'll become greedy at the core of your heart. If you worship some sinful habit, that same sin will grip your soul and poison your character to death. If you worship stuff, your life will become material, void of eternal significance. **If you give all your praise to the god of you, you'll become a disappointing little god to both yourself and to all those who trust in you."**

If you don't like who you're becoming you're worshipping the wrong things.

At some point each of us has to decide who will sit on the throne of our lives: us or God.

Here is what is so tricky about that decision. We mistakenly think that the way to find fulfillment and happiness is to live for ourselves, but that is a prescription for misery. And we mistakenly think that if we decide to live for God we're giving something up. But if you get back more than you gave up have you sacrificed anything at all? Jim Elliot said, **"He is no fool who loses what he cannot keep to gain what he cannot lose."**

If you live for yourself you'll end up **a disappointing little god** and **a miserable little person** because it's not what you were created to do. You weren't created to worship you. You were created to worship someone so much bigger and better than you. When you worship yourself your world becomes smaller and smaller. You're limited to you. And if you're anything like me you run out of stuff to worship pretty quick.

C.S. Lewis said, "The more we let God take us over, the more truly ourselves we become—because he made us. **He invented all the different people you and I were intended to be.** It is when I turn to Christ, when I give up myself to His personality, that I first begin to have a real personality of my own."

Wired for Worship

A *Newsweek* cover article, *God & the Brain: How We're Wired for Spirituality*, offers a fascinating look into the connection between neurology and spirituality. Kenneth Woodward says, **"Skeptics used to argue that anyone with half a brain should realize there is no God. Now scientists are telling us that one half of the brain, or a portion thereof, is 'wired' for religious experiences."**

Several centuries ago, William Shakespeare put it poetic terms, "The brain is the soul's fragile dwelling place."

According to neurotheology, the human mind is wired for worship. **Worshiping God is our deepest longing and**

highest calling.

In *The Air I Breathe*, Louis Giglio says, "**You my friend are a worshiper**! Everyday, all day long, in every place you worship. It's what you do. **It's who you are**. You cannot help but worship something. It's what you were made to do. Should you for some reason choose not to give God what He desires, you'll worship anyway—simply exchanging the Creator for something He has created. Worship happens everywhere all day long. **We all worship something all the time**."

You're wired to worship. God gave us eyes to see and ears to hear. God gave us a heart to pump blood throughout the body. And God gave us spirits to worship. You can't not worship. Everyone worships something.

"**So how do you know what you worship?**" Giglio asks, "It's easy. **You simply follow the trail of your time, your affection, your money, and your allegiance**." He says, "At the end of the trail you'll find a throne; and whatever or whoever is on that throne is what's of highest value to you. **On that throne is what you worship**."

Purple Mountain Majesty

G.K. Chesterton said that **his goal in life was to take nothing for granted**—not a sunrise, not a flower, not a laugh.

I think gratitude begins with a simple acknowledge that nothing belongs to us. And it ends with an appreciation for absolutely everything. Rick Warren says, "Every act of enjoyment becomes an act of worship when you thank God for it."

I recently flew to Colorado Springs to speak to a group of pastors and church planters. When I got into my rental car I didn't turn the radio on. I spent the entire drive from the airport to my hotel singing and praying and praising God. It's a miracle I got to the hotel. I couldn't keep my eyes on the road because I couldn't take my eyes off the mountains. They were absolutely breath-taking. The crown jewel is Pike's Peak. I got up at 4 AM the next morning and watched the sunrise paint the mountains pink and purple. It was that very mountain range that inspired Katherine Lee Bates to write *America the Beautiful* in 1893.

Here's what I blogged when I got back.

> *Do people who live in Colorado actually get used to the mountains?*
>
> *I think we tend to take our surroundings for granted. Washingtonians take the monuments for granted. Coloradoans take the mountains for granted. Minnesotans take lakes for granted. For some reason it's more enchanting seeing something you usually don't see or going someplace you usually don't go. So I was praising God because of the mountains but I think most people who live there stopped double-takes a long time ago! Such is human nature.*

We tend to take constants for granted. **Here is the problem with God: He is so good at what he does that we tend to take Him for granted**. He is so faithful. He is so available. He is so good. God is the ultimate constant so we take Him for granted.

When was the last time you prayed, "Lord, thanks for maintaining my body temperature right around 98.6. Thanks for purifying my toxins today. And thanks for helping my body convert that food into blood sugar. And, oh yah, thanks for hemoglobin!"

We don't pray like that, but I'm not sure we shouldn't. I just think we take way too much for granted.

John Donne said, **"There is nothing that God hath established in the constant course of Nature, and which** therefore is done everyday, but would seem a miracle, and exercise admiration, if it were done but once."

John Muir, the founder of the Sierra club, said, "**It is always sunrise somewhere.**"

I don't know why, but I'd never thought about that before I read it. It is always sunrise and sunset someplace! The miracle never ends. Someone is watching the sunrise in Maui and the sunset over the dessert dunes in Mauritania.

The challenge we face is this: we are surrounded by miracles but if we aren't careful we'll get used to them. Muir said, "This grand show is eternal. It is always sunrise somewhere; the dew is never all dried at once; a shower forever falling; vapor ever rising. Eternal sunrise, eternal sunset, eternal dawn, on seas and continents and islands, each in its turn, as the round earth rolls."

Eyes Wide Shut

Thomas Carlyle said, "**Worship is transcendent wonder.** Wonder for which there is no limit or measure; that is worship."

Carlyle said to imagine a man who had lived in a cave his entire life stepping outside for the first time to watch the sunrise. Carlyle said he would watch "with rapt astonishment the sight we daily witness with indifference."

G.K. Chesterton said, "Grown-up people are not strong enough to exult in monotony. Is it possible God says every morning, 'Do it again' to the sun; and every evening, 'Do it again' to the moon? The repetition in nature may not be a mere recurrence; it may be a theatrical encore."

The Message translation of Psalm 29 says, "**Bravo, God, Bravo. All the angels shout encore!**"

Philip Yancey says we need to experience two conversions. The first conversion is discovering the supernatural world. It is the realization that there is more to life than meets the eye! Yancey says the second conversion is rediscovering the natural world. We need to see the natural world through supernatural eyes. In other words, we need to look at creation and see it for what it really is—the handiwork of the Creator.

Leonardo Da Vinci said the average human "looks without seeing, listens without hearing, touches without feeling, eats without tasting, moves without physical awareness, inhales without awareness of odor or fragrance, and talks without thinking."

In other words, we go through the motions. Our eyes are wide shut.

That's the problem. Ephesians 1:18 is the solution. "I pray that the eyes of your heart may be enlightened in order that you may know the hope to which he has called you, the riches of his glorious inheritance in the saints, and his incomparably great power for us who believe."

The word "enlighten" means "**to see what was always there but you never noticed.**"

Genesis 28 is a classic example. Jacob wakes up from a God-ordained dream and he says, "**Surely the Lord is in this place and I was not aware of it.**"

One dimension of spiritual growth is an increasing awareness of God's presence. I Peter 1 says it this way. "**Your life is a journey, you must travel with a deep consciousness of God.**"

20/40 Vision

During my senior year of high school, my basketball coach noticed that I was squinting at the free throw line. He suggested that I go and get my eyes checked out. I had never worn contacts or glasses. I didn't think I needed them. But I went to the ophthalmologist and he said I had 20/40 vision which simply means I was seeing at 20 feet what most people could see at 40 feet. You can function pretty well with 20/40 vision—you can get your driver's license, you can read print, you can recognize faces. But you lack acuity—distant objects look blurry or fuzzy.

I will never forget the car ride home after putting in contacts for the first time. I almost can't put it into words. It was a five minute drive down 75th street in Naperville, Illinois. We had made that drive hundreds of times. But it was like I seeing things for the first time! I remember looking off to my right and seeing some pink and purple flowers. They were so vivid and so colorful and so beautiful I could hardly believe it. I was finally able to see what had always been there.

I love John Taylor's definition of being "in the spirit." He says, **"To be 'in the spirit' is to be vividly aware of everything that moment contains."**

The poet, Elizabeth Barrett Browning, said, "Earth is crammed with heaven, and every common bush afire with God; but only he who sees takes off his shoes; the rest sit around pluck blueberries."

First Day

Fredrick Buechner said, **"Today is the first day of you life because it has never been before and today is the last day of your life because it will never be again."**

Fredrick Buechner said that everyday he woke up it was like God said, "Let there be Buechner."

What a great way to start the day!

Every day should be experienced as if it is the first day and last day of your life. It never has been before and it never will be again.

Someone recently told me about a friend of theirs who had never seen snow before. The first snowflakes they'd ever seen starting falling around 3 AM. This friend went outside in the middle of the night to play in the snow. He didn't realize the snow was cold so his body got numb pretty quickly, but not before experiencing snow for the first time. There is something so special and so unique about the first time we experience something.

I'll never forget the first time Lora and I held hands. I remember exactly where we were because that experience is seared into my memory. It was like electricity shooting through my hand and into the rest of my body!

I remember my first flight. I looked out the window almost the entire flight because I'd never experienced anything like it before!

The first time you see something or do something there is an added element of excitement.

M.J. Ryan says, "The secret to love—and a sense of joy and gratitude toward all of life—**is to see, feel, and hear as if for the first time. Before the scales of the habitual clouded the brilliant blue sky outside your office window, the tangy juiciness of an orange, or the softness of a loved one's hands.** Before you got used to her kind words, his musical laughter, that they became invisible."

Last Day

In his book, *Rumors*, Philip Yancey tells a story about a friend of his who was going blind. The doctors told her she would lose her sight so she decided to revisit all of her favorite places to see them one more time before she went blind. **It's not until we lose what we have that we really appreciate it.** It is retroactive gratitude.

We need to see as if we're going blind. We need to hear as if we're going deaf. We need to live as if we're dying.

The 17th century Anglican poet, George Herbert said, "You have given me so much. Give me one more thing—a grateful heart."

God isn't as concerned with our **level of righteousness** as He is our **level of gratitude**. Jesus tells a story in Luke 7 with an interesting twist. He says that **those who have sinned a lot have an advantage over those who have sinned a little.** Jesus asks Peter who was more grateful—the person who had been forgiven a small debt or the person who has been forgiven a large debt? It's a no-brainer. **What you can do for God isn't nearly as important as simply appreciating what God has done for you!**

The Elephant Man

John Merrick was born in 1863 with a medical condition known as neurofibromatosis. In short, John Merrick may have been the most deformed human being in history. At the age of four he was abandoned by his mother. At the age of fourteen a traveling carnival turned him into a human freak show. He was treated like a circus animal. People would pay to get into the show and then shriek in horror when they saw him.

One day a surgeon named Frederick Treves wandered into the carnival, paid a shilling to watch the show, and could hardly believe what he saw. Treves said, "He was the most disgusting specimen of humanity that I have ever seen."

Dr. Treves arranged to have John Merrick examined and he detailed Merrick's deformities: a bony mass protruding from his brow; spongy skin; a misshapen head the circumference of a man's waist; the mouth a distorted slobbering aperture; the nose a dangling lump of skin; his right arm overgrown to twice its normal size, its fingers stubby and useless; and deformed legs that can not support his body weight.

After the examination, Treves tried to communicate with Merrick but because of his mouth deformities, Merrick's speech was unintelligible. Treves assumed he was an imbecile. Treves gave him his card, told him to contact him if he could be of assistance, and returned him to the custody of the carnival.

Several years later, the police found Merrick in a dark corner at a London train station muttering words they couldn't understand. But they found a card with the name of

Dr. Frederick Treves. They notified him and Treves found Merrick huddled in a corner whimpering like a little baby. He took him back to the hospital and ordered a tray of food, but the nurse who delivered it screamed when she saw Merrick, dropped the tray, and ran out of the room.

Over time the hospital staff became accustomed to the sight and Treves learned to decipher Merrick's speech. He discovered that Merrick was anything but an imbecile. In fact, he was a voracious reader of Scripture. Treves took care of Merrick the rest of his life.

One day he arranged for a woman to enter his room, smile at him, wish him a good morning, and shake his hand. Treves said, "The effect upon Merrick was not quite what I had expected. As he let go of her hand he bent his head on his knees and sobbed until I thought he would never cease. He told me afterwards that this was the first woman who had ever smiled at him, and the first woman in his whole life, who had shaken hands with him." Treves said it was a turning point. "He began to change little by little from a hunted thing into a man."

Treves arranged to smuggle Merrick into private boxes of London theaters to see plays. He gave him books to read. And he introduced him to the world of nature. Merrick loved to listen to songbirds, flush rabbits, and pick wildflowers. Treves said that to each new experience Merrick responded by saying, **"I am happy every hour of the day."**

John Merrick, better known as The Elephant Man, died at twenty-seven years of age, but not before inspiring those who could look past his deformities and see his heart.

You've already read Dr. Treves' description of John Merrick's physical deformities. Listen to his description of John Merrick's soul. "His troubles have ennobled him. He showed himself to be a gentle, affectionate and lovable creature without a grievance and without an unkind word for anyone. **I have never heard him complain.** I have never heard him deplore his ruined life or resent the treatment he had received at the hands of callous keepers."

Treves was absolutely mystified by Merrick. He was robbed of his childhood. He was treated like a wild beast. Yet he emerged with such a pure heart. John Merrick wrote a poem that he would often recite to guests.

> *Tis true my form is something odd*
> *But blaming me is blaming God*
> *Could I create myself anew*
> *I would not fail in pleasing you*
> *If I could reach from pole to pole*
> *I would be measured by the soul*

Was John Merrick deformed? Or was John Merrick what all of us should aspire to?

Everyone's life is full of bumps and bruises, but I'm not sure any of our lives even begin to approximate the mental and spiritual and emotional anguish that John Merrick endured. Merrick most certainly walked through valleys of doubt and despair like all of us, but somehow he was able to say, "I am happy every hour of the day."

The Apostle Paul had an impressive resume of pain and suffering. He said in Philippians 4:12, "I know what it is to be in need and I know what it is to have plenty. I have learned the secret of being content in any and every situation."

Happiness

Blaise Pascal said, "All men seek happiness." C.S. took it a step further. "It is a Christian duty for everyone to be as happy as he can."

All of us want to be happy, but happiness is so elusive. It seems like a rapidly moving target. I can tell you this: you don't find it by looking for it.

Here's a definition of sin. **Sin is seeking happiness**

where no lasting happiness can be found—outside a relationship with God. It's a futile attempt to meet a legitimate need in illegitimate ways.

Stop and think about this: **if you always acted in your best interest you would always obey God**. Sin is short-changing yourself and God. You settle for something less than best.

Lewis said that human history is a record of man's attempt to find happiness outside of God. We may find temporary happiness, but not the infinite joy we crave. "God invented us as man invents an engine. A car is made to run on gasoline, and it would not properly run on anything else. **God designed the human machine to run on Himself**. He Himself is the fuel our spirits were designed to burn."

My kids have a toy with different shaped pieces of plastic—squares, triangles, circles. And each of those shapes fits through a corresponding hole. The square shape fits in the square hole. The triangle shape fits in the triangle hole. I have to admit, the thing drives me crazy! It is so obvious from my vantage point what shape goes in what hole. But toddlers will try to jam a square in the circle-shaped hole or the triangle in the triangle-shaped hole. I want to grab the toy, stuff the right shapes in the right holes, and get on with the next toy!

Augustine said, "**There is a God-shaped vacuum in every human heart**."

I wonder if God gets frustrated watching us try to jam things into the God-shaped hole in our heart? There is only one thing that will fill the God-shaped hole in your heart—God.

We mistakenly think that seeking God will somehow narrow our lives, but it has the opposite effect.

G.K. Chesterton said, "How much happier you would be, how much more of you there would be, if the hammer of a *Higher God* could smash your small cosmos."

Superman

Nothing is more dangerous than a low view of God. Nothing is more important than a high view of God. But we tend to **overestimate ourselves** and **underestimate God**.

When Mohammed Ali was the Heavyweight Champion of the world he wasn't lacking for confidence. On one particular flight from Chicago to Las Vegas, a flight attendant did the normal rounds to make sure seat belts were fastened before takeoff. Ali was unbuckled. The flight attendant said, "Mr. Ali, we're about ready to take off, could you please fasten your seatbelt?" Mohammed Ali said, "Superman don't need no seatbelt." Without skipping a beat, the flight attendant said, "Superman don't need no airplane."

In his book, *Saints and Madmen*, Russell Shorto, makes a fascinating distinction between mystics and psychotics. He writes, "**A mystic is humbled by his experience**, a **psychotic is inflated**." The psychological term is grandiosity. The psychotic becomes pride-full and self-absorbed. But the mystic is humbled and becomes acutely aware of his smallness.

"**The chief proof of a man's real greatness**," observed Sherlock Holmes, "**lies in the perception of his smallness**."

President Theodore Roosevelt had an interesting ritual when he occupied the White House. He would occasionally go outside and look up into the night sky with his naturalist friend, William Beebe. They would locate a faint spot of light in the lower left-hand corner of Pegasus and recite the following: "That is the Spiral Galaxy of Andromeda. It is as large as our Milky Way. It is one of a hundred million galaxies. It is seven hundred and fifty thousand light years away. It consists of a hundred billion suns, each larger than our own sun." The President would pause and grin. And he would say, "**Now I think we feel small enough**. Let's go to bed."

Overestimating ourselves is a problem. **Underestimating God** is an even bigger problem. And all of us do it. We can't not. Ephesians 3:20 says that God is "**able to do immeasurably more than all we can ask or imagine.**" God doesn't fit within the confines of the cerebral cortex. Our **left-brains** can't reduce Him to a mathematical formula. Our **right-brains** can't reduce Him to a combination of the twenty-six letters of the English language. He is **the Irreducible One**. He defies human imagination.

So what do we do?

We shrink God to four dimensions of spacetime. We bring God down to our level. The technical term is anthropomorphism. Instead of allowing God to recreate us in His image, we recreate God in our image. And, in the words of A.W. Tozer, "**The end result is a God who can never surprise us, never astonish us, never overwhelm us, never transcend us.**"

Measureless

William Jennings Bryan, now famous for his role as prosecutor in the Scopes Monkey Trial, used to talk about the mystery of God using the image of a watermelon.

> *I have observed the power of the watermelon seed. It has the power of drawing from the ground and through itself 200,000 times its weight. When you can tell me how it takes this material and out of it colors an outside surface beyond the imitation of art, and then forms inside of it a white rind and within that again a red heart, thickly inlaid with black seeds, each one of which in turn is capable of drawing through itself 200,000 times its weight—when you can explain to me the mystery of the watermelon, you can ask me to explain the mystery of God.*

According to one count, there are about 100 million species of plants, animals, and microorganisms on earth. Only about 1.4 million species have been sufficiently studied to be given scientific names! That means **98.6 percent of God's creation remains a mystery!** We know so much, yet we know so little.

Naturalist Edward Wilson says, "**Our sense of wonder grows exponentially: the greater the knowledge, the deeper the mystery.**"

It's true of creation. It's true of the Creator. The greater the knowledge the deeper the mystery, and that makes us uncomfortable.

We can manage what we can measure. Measurement is one way we try to exercise control. So it's no wonder we are measurement freaks. We measure money in dollars, time in minutes, height in inches, and weight in pounds. We measure wind and rain and snow. We measure the height of mountains and the depth of oceans. We measure sound and light and energy. We measure earthquakes and hurricanes. We measure atoms and galaxies. No matter how big or how small, we measure it.

In case it comes up in *Trivial Pursuit*, the circumference of the earth is 24,859 miles. On July 3, 1990, the earth was 94,508,105 miles from the sun. Absolute zero, theoretically the lowest possible temperature, is –273 degrees Celsius. Escape velocity, the speed needed to escape the gravitation pull of planet earth, is 17,500 mph.

You get the point: **we measure everything. Everything, that is, except God.**

Romans 11:33 says, "Oh, the depth of the riches of the wisdom and knowledge of God! How unsearchable his judgments, and his paths beyond tracing out!"

His wisdom is measureless.

Ephesians 3:18 says, "I pray that you might have the power to know how *wide and long and high and deep* is the love of Christ, and to know this love that *surpasses* knowledge."

His love is measureless.

Ephesians 3:20 says, "Now to Him who is able to do immeasurably more than all we can ask or imagine, according to his power that is at work within us."

His power is measureless.

Romans 5:20 says, "But where sin increased, grace increased all the more."

Sin has its limits. But God's grace is measureless!

12.3 Billion Light Years

My theological touchstone is Isaiah 55:8. The Lord says, "My thoughts are not your thoughts, neither are my ways your ways. **As the heavens are higher than the earth** so are my ways higher than your ways, and my thoughts than your thoughts."

Spatial distances are almost incomprehensible, but let me give it a shot. Light travels at **186,000 miles per second**. Light waves are so fast that you can have a real-time conversation with someone halfway around the world. The sun is approximately 93,000,000 miles from Earth. If you got into your car and started driving 65 mph, twenty-four hours a day, it'd be a 163 year trip! But traveling at the speed of light, our sunshine is only 8 minutes old.

Stick with me.

Astronomers have discovered galaxies **12.3 billion light-years away**. That means it takes light, traveling at **186,000 miles per second**, more than twelve billion years to reach the outer edges of space. And God says in Isaiah 55:8: that's about the distance between our thoughts and His thoughts.

I'm not saying you can't know God. You can. But Psalm 145:3 says, "There are no boundaries to His greatness; **His greatness no one can fathom.**"

You underestimate God by approximately 12.3 billion light-years!

Sometimes we analyze and categorize and theorize instead of just letting God be God. I think God is looking for people who don't tell Him what He can't do. Mark Nepo said, **"Birds don't need ornithologists to fly."** Birds don't need ornithologists to fly and God doesn't need theologians to do miracles!

God knows no boundaries. He isn't limited to four dimensions of spacetime.

Psalm 36 says, "His love is meteoric, his loyalty astronomic, His purpose titanic, His verdicts oceanic. Yet in His largeness, nothing gets lost" (*The Message*).

Epilogue

In *Man's Search for Meaning*, Viktor Frankl recounts his experiences in a Nazi concentration camp during World War II. One of the first things the captors did was strip the prisoners of their personal effects—wedding rings, pictures, medals. Even their names were taken away and replaced with a number—Number 119,104 in the case of Frankl. Frankl recalls his first day this way, "While we were waiting for the shower, our nakedness was brought home to us: we really had nothing now except our bare bodies—even minus hair; **all we possessed, literally, was our naked existence.**"

The Nazi captors tried to strip Frankl of his individuality, but it had the opposite effect. He emerged with a renewed appreciation for the "uniqueness and singleness" of every individual. "**When the impossibility of replacing a person is realized, it allows the responsibility which a man has for his existence and its continuance to appear in all its magnitude.**"

Frankl concluded, "He who knows the 'why' for his existence, will be able to bear almost any 'how'."

When everything is stripped away, who are you?

Time After Time

The book of Revelation is a prophetic description of time after time.

Revelation 2:17 says, "He who has an ear let him hear what the Spirit says to the churches. To him who overcomes, I will give some of the hidden manna. I will also give him **a white stone** with **a new name written on it, known only to him who receives it**."

You will be you in heaven. You will, in some form or fashion, retain your earthly identity. You will have your memories, your personality, your relationships, your gifts, your dreams. I don't think God will take those away. But I think you will become who you were meant to be in the truest and fullest sense.

I Corinthians 13:12 says, "Now we see but **a poor reflection** as in a mirror; then we shall see **face to face.** Now I know **in part**; then I shall **know fully**, even as I am **fully known**."

It will be like an **artist's unveiling**. God will reveal who we really are!

It's hard to imagine because there is nothing to compare it to, but I think **it will be like meeting ourselves for the first time!**

True Name

John Eldredge says, "The history of a man's relationship with God is the story of how God calls him out, takes him on a journey and **gives him his true name**."

My name is Mark Allan Batterson, but that isn't my real name. That is just a name given to me by my **earthly parents**. My **true name** is the **new name** that will be given to me by my **Heavenly Father**.

And that moment—the moment we hear God say our new name for the first time—will be the most amazing moment any of us has ever experienced. **Time will literally**

stand still because it will be **time after time**. Our lives will make perfect sense in that moment. God will reveal the true you—who you were meant to be and who you will be in eternity.

Unique

It's easy to feel small and insignificant when you're one of six billion people roaming the planet. What difference do I make?

Let me put it in **human terms**. If you said that two out of my three kids would love me, do you think that'd be good enough for me? No way! Each of my children is invaluable and irreplaceable.

I have a confession to make. **I don't love my kids the same**. No one does! Each of my children is unique and **I love them uniquely**.

In the same sense, God doesn't love us the same. Sure, his love is unconditional and unchangeable. But God doesn't love us the same. **God loves us uniquely**. God finds joy in each unique expression of worship.

There never has been and never will be anyone like you. That isn't a testament to you. It's a testament to the God who created you.

The significance of uniqueness is this: **no one else can worship God like you**.

No one can take your place.

About the Author

 ⋅⊱≒◉⊆⋅

Mark Batterson serves as Lead Pastor of National Community Church located in Washington, DC. NCC is a creative and innovate congregation reaching emerging generations. The congregation is 80% single and 80% twenty-something.

Starting with a core group of 19 people meeting in a DC public school, NCC has morphed into one church with two locations—the movie theaters @ Union Station and the movie theaters @ Ballston Common Mall.

The macro vision of NCC is to meet in movie theaters @ metro stops throughout the DC metropolitan area.

To learn more about NCC, go to www.theaterchurch.com.

Mark is the originator of evotional.com. His weekly evotional has grown to more than 2,000 readers worldwide since 2002.

For a free evotional subscription or additional resources, go to www.evotional.com.

Mark is an adjunct faculty member at Regent University (DC campus). His area of expertise is creative communication and ministry in the postmodern matrix. He also speaks to pastors and church planters in a variety of conference and seminar settings.

Mark has lived on Capitol Hill with his wife, Lora, since 1996. They have three children—Parker, Summer, and Josiah.

Printed in the United States
67957LVS00002B/116